SRA
DIFFERENTIATED INSTRUCTION

aligned with
Language for Learning

McGraw Hill **SRA**

Columbus, OH

Acknowledgments:

The publisher would like to thank Dr. Betsy Loveday;

Angela Przychodzin-Havis, M.Ed.; and Jorge E. Gonzalez, Ph.D.;

for their help in preparing *Differentiated Instruction*.

SRAonline.com

Printed in the United States of America.

Send all inquiries to this address:
SRA/McGraw-Hill
4400 Easton Commons
Columbus, OH 43219

ISBN: 978-0-07-609452-3
MHID: 0-07-609452-9

6 7 8 9 10 11 QVS 23 22 21 20 19

The *McGraw-Hill* Companies

TABLE OF CONTENTS

INTRODUCTION

What is Differentiated Instruction?

Differentiated instruction is targeted instruction for specific students in need of additional support. The purpose of differentiated instruction is to individualize instruction so that all children meet the instructional objectives. It is instruction that is planned and delivered with precision in small, flexible groups of children. These small groups are important in order to reinforce and review skills explicitly and systematically based on children's needs as determined by assessment results.

How is Differentiated Instruction Achieved?

The activities in Differentiated Instruction provide additional review of the skills featured in the Language for Learning program. Included at the point of use in the four Language for Learning Presentation Books are fifteen assessments. Following each assessment, directions are given for differentiating instruction for children who need extra help based on their assessment results.

The material in this book is designed to augment the existing instructional tools with activities, stories, poems, and games. These items have been collected from throughout the program and include reviews of skills from Language Activity Masters Books 1 and 2, the Picture Cards User's Guide, and the Expanded Language Activities and Storybooks from the four Presentation Books. This book also includes additional activities that have been designed to coincide with and reinforce the skills children are learning in the classroom.

How is Differentiated Instruction Organized?

The charts included in this Differentiated Instruction book are composed of three separate sections: Activities for Additional Support for children approaching mastery; Enrichment Activities for children at mastery; and Tips for Teachers and Home Connections for children who are learning English (English Language Learners, or ELL).

The charts themselves are further broken down according to the parts of each assessment. For example, Assessment 6 includes five parts: Information, Classification, Plurals, Tense, and Concept Application. The differentiated instruction activities for this assessment have been written to coincide with these parts. This separation enables you to explicitly and systematically target those areas of difficulty with activities and games that will review those specific skills. Based on individual results of the assessments, you will know exactly which skills children are struggling with, and you will be armed with a set of resources to target those skills only, thereby maximizing the efficiency of instructional time.

DIFFERENTIATED INSTRUCTION

Activities for Additional Support

Approaching Mastery

Children who score below 90 percent or groups that average below 80 percent

Following Assessment 1, Part A—Information
- Take pictures of children, or have them bring pictures from home. Have children identify the person whose picture you hold up (Expanded Language Activities for lessons 6–10, page v).
- Play Who Is Missing? Have children close their eyes while one child moves out of sight. Children open their eyes and try to name the child who is missing.
- Have children sing "What Is Your Name?" using each child's name. Vary the activity to include the school's and teacher's names.

Following Assessment 1, Part B—Actions
- Play Simon says using the actions children are learning (Expanded Language Activities for lessons 1–5, page v).
- Play Mother, May I? Choose a child to be Mother. Give the child a picture to hold of someone doing an action they have learned. Children say, "Mother, may I stand up?" Mother says, "Yes, you may." (Children stand up.) Allow Mother to pick a new Mother and repeat the game using different pictures (Expanded Language Activities for lessons 11–15, page v).
- Use Picture Cards 6 and 8. Have each child choose a card, act out the card, and then say the whole thing. Repeat with each card.

Following Assessment 1, Part C—Object Identification
- Have children cut out pictures of common objects they are learning (Expanded Language Activities for lessons 6–10, page v).
- Using real or play objects—ball, book, and so on—have children identify each object and then say the whole thing, such as "This is a ball."
- Using Picture Cards 13, 16, 18, 43, 45, 77, 79, 80, 84, 87, 90, 97, 100, 104, 112, 119, 122, 128, 132, 146, 147, 152, 153, 156, 159, and 160, have children identify the picture and then say the whole thing, such as "This is a ball."

Enrichment Activities

At Mastery

Children who score at or above 90 percent

Following Assessment 1, Part A—Information
- Read aloud *The Three Little Pigs* (Expanded Language Activities for lessons 1–5, page v).
- Read aloud *Goldilocks and the Three Bears*. Have children role-play the story (Expanded Language Activities for lessons 6–10, page v).
- Take pictures of your school from different viewpoints. Show the pictures, and have children name the school.

Following Assessment 1, Part B—Actions
- Play Roll the Cube! Actions Block (Language Activity Masters Book 1, lesson 10).
- Read aloud *The Three Little Pigs*. Have children role-play the story (Expanded Language Activities for lessons 6–10, page v).
- Read aloud *Here Are My Hands* by Bill Martin Jr. Have children act out the story.

Following Assessment 1, Part C—Object Identification
- Read aloud *Goodnight Moon*. Have children identify various objects in the story (Expanded Language Activities for lessons 1–5, page v).
- Play Tic-Tac-Toe, Three in a Row (Language Activity Masters Book 2, lesson 5).
- Play Object Concentration Game (Language Activity Masters Book 1, lesson 5).
- Have children make booklets of pictures and tell stories about the booklets (Expanded Language Activities for lessons 6–10, page v).
- Select magazines or books appropriate for the class. Have children find pictures of common objects they have learned and make up statements about them.

Tips for Teachers

English Language Learners	• See Extra Help guidelines for children who score below 90 percent or groups that average below 80 percent on Assessment 1. • See Expanded Language Activities on page v in Presentation Book A. • Label classroom objects in English and, when available, in children's native languages (parents are a valuable asset in this activity). • Describe and model the mouth formations for words, and then guide children while practicing with a mirror. • Incorporate "First you say _____; then you say _____; now say it fast" activities throughout the day. For example, say the beginning sound and the rest of the word, and then say it fast for such lesson words as classmates' names and classroom objects. • Show realia (for example, a cup, a banana, or a chair) or other visuals (for example, a photograph of fish) of objects or concepts. • Have children make picture dictionaries by cutting out pictures from magazines or newspapers. • Use primary language equivalents when available, and then ask children to say the words in English.

Home Connections

- Encourage children to share their completed workbook pages with their families.
- Provide an audiotape to use with picture flash cards of common objects taught (for example, tree, dog, shoe, and cat).
- Encourage children to practice mouth formations with a mirror at home.
- Encourage parents to help children identify realia and other visuals of common objects at home.
- Encourage parents to ask children the names of their school, teacher, classmates, classroom objects, and body parts.
- Encourage parents to read to their children or tell them a story using the pictures from the book, asking them questions about the story. Encourage children to respond in complete sentences.
- Have parents make a Word Wall of words their child is having difficulty with.

Assessment 2 (Lessons 11–20)

Activities for Additional Support

Approaching Mastery Children who score below 90 percent or groups that average below 80 percent	**Following Assessment 2, Part A—Information** • Have children sit in a circle, and teach them "Polly Put the Kettle On." Point to different children as the group sings, and substitute the names of children for *Polly* (Expanded Language Activities for lessons 16–20, page v). • Play Who Ate the Cookies from the Cookie Jar? Use this game when children are lining up for various activities. Start the game by naming one child, saying, "Who ate the cookies from the cookie jar? _____ ate the cookies from the cookie jar." The named child gets into line and responds, "Who, me?" Other children respond, "Yes, you. _____ ate the cookies from the cookie jar." The named child responds, "Not me." The class responds, "Then who?" The named child then identifies another child in the class. Play until all children are in line. **Following Assessment 2, Part B—Actions** • Play Simon says with actions children are learning (Expanded Language Activities for lessons 11–15, page v). • Use the Fold-A-Monkey Hand Puppet, and sing the song "Five Little Monkeys." Start the song with five little monkeys jumping on the bed. Then change the rhyme to eating, sleeping, sitting, and standing. Children can use their fingers or other parts of their bodies to dramatize the actions (Language Activity Masters Book 2, lesson 20).

Activities for Additional Support

Following Assessment 2, Part C—Common Objects

- Using Picture Cards 13, 15, 16, 18, 22, 24, 28, 34, 43 ,45, 47, 77, 79, 80, 81, 82, 83, 84, 87, 97, 100, 102, 104, 112, 119, 122, 127, 128, 132, 146, 147, 148, 149, 150, 151, 152, 153, 156, 160, 188, 190, 192, and 200, have children identify the picture and then say the whole thing, such as "This is a deer."
- Read aloud *Goodnight Moon.* Children say the words with you (Expanded Language Activities for lessons 16–20, page v).

Following Assessment 2, Part D—Identity Statements

- Play Hot Potato Object Pass. With children seated in a circle, pass out several assorted small objects (ball, box, clock, toy, bus, and so on). Play music for short intervals. When the music stops, each child holding an object identifies it and says the whole thing.
- Play bingo using objects children have learned to identify (Expanded Language Activities for lessons 16–20, page v).
- Trace an outline of each child onto butcher paper. Have children identify body parts and color the picture. Have each child identify each picture (Expanded Language Activities for lessons 11–15, page v).

Following Assessment 2, Part E—Action Statements

- Play Mother, May I? using actions children are learning (Expanded Language Activities for lessons 16–20, page v).
- Play Hokey Pokey using actions children are learning (Expanded Language Activities for lessons 16–20, page v).

Enrichment Activities

At Mastery

Children who score at or above 90 percent

Following Assessment 2, Part A—Information

- Read aloud *Goldilocks and the Three Bears.* Have children join in as you read the bears' lines (Expanded Language Activities for lessons 11–15, page v).
- Read aloud *The Three Little Pigs.* Have children join in as you read the pigs' and the wolf's lines (Expanded Language Activities for lessons 11–15, page v).
- Play the Whose Shoe? Guessing Game. Have each child in the group remove one shoe and place it in a shoe pile. Hold up one shoe from the pile, and ask, "Whose shoe?" Children say the first and last names of the matching-shoe owner (a version of Language Activity Masters Book 1, lesson 30).

Following Assessment 2, Part B—Actions

- Play Action Antics. This is a charades game using action verbs. Find or draw simple pictures of a person standing, sitting, sleeping, eating, and jumping. Place the pictures facedown, and have a child pick a picture without showing the class. The child then acts out the action for his or her classmates to guess. Whoever labels the action correctly and can say the whole thing becomes "It."

Following Assessment 2, Part C—Common Objects

- Have children look through magazines, cut out familiar objects, and paste them onto construction paper. Then ask the group, "What is this?" (Expanded Language Activities for lessons 11–15, page v).
- Play bingo using objects children have learned to identify (Expanded Language Activities for lessons 16–20, page v).
- Use A House Is a House for Me Magic Book (Language Activity Masters Book 2, lesson 15).

Following Assessment 2, Part D—Identity Statements

- Play Road Race! (Language Activity Masters Book 1, lesson 15).
- Play The People on the Bus (Language Activity Masters Book 1, lesson 20).

Following Assessment 2, Part E—Action Statements

- Read aloud *There Was an Old Woman Who Swallowed a Fly.* Have children role-play the story (Expanded Language Activities for lessons 11–15, page v).

Tips for Teachers

English Language Learners	• See Extra Help guidelines for children who score below 90 percent or groups that average below 80 percent on Assessment 2. • See Expanded Language Activities on page v in Presentation Book A. • Continue labeling classroom objects in English and, when available, in children's native languages. • Play the guessing game What's Missing? by setting out two to three known objects. Cover the objects with a cloth, remove the cloth, and give children a few minutes to look at the objects. Have children cover their eyes while you remove one object, and then have children guess which object was removed. Allow children who guessed correctly to remove the next object. • Incorporate "First you say _____; then you say _____; now say it fast" activities throughout the day. For example, say the beginning sound, the rest of the word, and then say it fast for such lesson words as *flag, bicycle,* and *house.* Also review any words that children had difficulty with from previous lessons. • Describe and model the mouth formations for words, and then guide children while practicing with a mirror. • Show realia (for example, bookcase, shirt, or box) or other visuals (for example, photograph of bus) of objects or concepts. • Have children add to their picture dictionaries by cutting out pictures from magazines or newspapers. Then play the You Be the Teacher game by having children take turns being the teacher and asking others "What does _____ mean?" • Use primary language equivalents when available, and then ask children to say the words in English.

Home Connections

• Encourage children to share their completed workbook pages with their families.
• Provide an audiotape to use with picture flash cards of common objects taught (for example, bus, bookcase, bicycle, and clock).
• Encourage children to practice mouth formations with a mirror at home.
• Encourage parents to help children identify realia and other visuals of common objects at home.
• Provide an audiotape of "First you say _____; then you say _____; now say it fast" activities, and encourage parents to help children practice other similar activities throughout the day. Encourage children to practice with a mirror at home as needed.
• Encourage parents to help children practice using primary language equivalents and English words wh en possible.
• Encourage parents to read to their children or tell them a story using the pictures from the book, asking them questions about the story. Encourage children to respond in complete sentences.
• Encourage parents to continue adding words their child is having difficulty with to his or her Word Wall.

Activities for Additional Support

Approaching Mastery

Children who score below 90 percent or groups that average below 80 percent

Following Assessment 3, Part A—Information

- Have children identify their neighbor (seated in a circle). Each child has to repeat the names of all of the preceding children (Expanded Language Activities for lessons 21–25, page vi).
- Sing "Do You Know the Muffin Man?" The group can sing this familiar song substituting a child's first and last name for "the Muffin Man," and use the name of the city or town where children live.
- Play Doggy, Doggy, Where's Your Bone? Select one child to be the "doggy" who turns away from the group while the teacher hands a "bone" (small, easily concealed object) to another child in the group. Children then sing the song below as the "doggy" thinks about which child may be hiding the bone. The "doggy" has three tries to pick the holder of the "bone" and to say the first and last name of each child guessed.

> Children: *Doggy, Doggy, where's your bone?*
> *Someone stole it from your home.*
> Doggy: *Was it* (first name, last name)?
> *Was it* (first name, last name)?
> *Was it* (first name, last name)?

Following Assessment 3, Part B—Identity Statements

- Read "Polly and the Lion" to children, and have them respond to questions about the story and repeat what Polly says (Presentation Book A, Storybook 1, page 1).
- Read the poem "My Cat, My Dog, My Frog," and have children respond as you touch the pictures and ask the questions at the end (Presentation Book A, Storybook 1, page 6).
- Read "Dozy, Bring a Hamburger" to children, and have them respond to questions about the story and repeat what Dad and Dozy say (Presentation Book A, Storybook 1, page 7).
- Use the "I Love My Cat" poem and puppets (Language Activity Masters Book 2, lesson 25).

Following Assessment 3, Part C—Actions—First, Next

- Read aloud *The Three Little Pigs*. Have children identify what each character did first and next.
- Have children respond to first and next directions such as "First touch your nose; next touch your head" by completing the action.

Following Assessment 3, Part D—Actions—Pronouns

- Have children cut out pictures of people doing actions. Paste the pictures onto construction paper. As the group pantomimes the actions, call on different children to name the actions (Expanded Language Activities for lessons 26–30, page vi).
- Read *Brown Bear, Brown Bear, What Do You See?* Have children reread the story in parts (Expanded Language Activities for lessons 26–30, page vi).

Following Assessment 3, Part E—Action Statements

- Use Picture Cards 1 through 9. Show a card, and ask children what the person is doing. Children respond with "This _____ is _____."

Enrichment Activities

At Mastery

Children who score at or above 90 percent

Following Assessment 3, Part A—Information

- Play Whose Shoe? (Language Activity Masters Book 1, lesson 30).
- Play Beanbag Toss by drawing lines to separate a large piece of butcher paper into quarters. In each quarter, draw pictures of one of the following: several children, the teacher, the school, the city/town in which children live. Have children take turns throwing a beanbag onto a picture. They must say the name of the picture on which the beanbag lands.

Following Assessment 3, Part B—Identity Statements

- Read "Polly and the Lion" to children, and have them respond to questions about the story, repeat what Polly says, and role-play (Presentation Book A, Storybook 1, page 1).
- Use Peek at the Pictures (Language Activity Masters Book 1, lesson 25).

Enrichment Activities

- Read the poem "My Cat, My Dog, My Frog," and have children respond as you touch the pictures. Ask the questions at the end, and call on individual children to repeat the entire poem (Presentation Book A, Storybook 1, page 6).
- Read "Dozy, Bring a Hamburger" to children, and have them respond to questions about the story, repeat what Dad says, and role-play (Presentation Book A, Storybook 1, page 7).
- Use the "I Love My Cat" poem and puppets (Language Activity Masters Book 2, lesson 25).

Following Assessment 3, Part C—Actions—First, Next
- Read aloud *The Three Little Pigs.* Have children identify and role-play what each character did first and next.

Following Assessment 3, Part D—Actions—Pronouns
- Have a grab bag of illustrated actions. A child picks one and performs the action. The rest of the group tells what the child is doing (Expanded Language Activities for lessons 26–30, page vi).
- Read *Brown Bear, Brown Bear, What Do You See?* Have children role play what "I" see and what "you" see (Expanded Language Activities for lessons 26–30, page vi).

Following Assessment 3, Part E—Action Statements
- Use Picture Cards 1 through 9. Show a card, and ask children what the person is doing. Children respond with "This _____ is _____." Next, show another card, and ask children if the person is doing _____. Make sure that the action you state is NOT the action being performed. Children respond with "This _____ is **not** _____."

Tips for Teachers

English Language Learners

- See Extra Help guidelines for children who score below 90 percent or groups that average below 80 percent on Assessment 3.
- See Expanded Language Activities on page vi in Presentation Book A.
- Continue labeling classroom objects in English and, when available, in children's native languages.
- Play What's Missing?, and allow children who guessed correctly to remove the next object. Gradually increase the number of objects when children are ready.
- Describe and model mouth formations for words in "Say it slowly; say it fast" activities, and then guide children while practicing with a mirror.
- Show realia or other visuals of objects and concepts (for example, pictures of people eating, sleeping, or jumping).
- Encourage children to use new words at home. The next day, ask, "Did anyone share the words at home?"
- Practice asking children "yes or no" questions about everyday objects in the classroom. For example, point to a chair, and ask, "Is this a hat?"
- Reinforce the concept of opposites by showing other examples of "full" and "not full" and "wet" and "not wet." For example, show an empty jar, and then fill the jar with marbles or other classroom manipulatives.
- Use Total Physical Response (TPR) to show concepts of pronouns by saying a word or phrase and then demonstrating the concept by pantomiming or gesturing. For example, say, "This is your shoe"; then point to a child's shoe. Guide children as they use TPR to demonstrate the concept.
- Have children add to their picture dictionaries by cutting out pictures from magazines or newspapers. Then play the You Be the Teacher game by having children take turns being the teacher and asking others "What does _____ mean?"
- Use primary language equivalents when available, and then ask children to say the words in English.

Home Connections

- Encourage children to share their completed workbook pages with their families.
- Provide an audiotape to use with picture flash cards of common objects and actions taught (for example, balloon, telephone, swimming, and jumping).
- Encourage children to practice mouth formations with a mirror at home.
- Encourage parents to help children identify realia and other visuals of common objects at home.
- Encourage parents to incorporate "Say it slowly; say it fast" activities throughout the day. Encourage children to practice with a mirror at home as needed.
- Encourage parents to play the What's Missing? game at home.
- Encourage parents to ask children the name of their town, city, or area.
- Encourage parents to help children practice using primary language equivalents and English words when possible.
- Encourage parents to read to their children or tell them a story using the pictures from the book, asking them questions about the story. Encourage children to respond in complete sentences.
- Encourage parents to continue adding words their child is having difficulty with to his or her Word Wall.

Assessment 4 (Lessons 31–40)

Approaching Mastery

Children who score below 90 percent or groups that average below 80 percent

Activities for Additional Support

Following Assessment 4, Part A—Information

- Sing the song "Count the Days" to the tune of "Twinkle, Twinkle, Little Star."
    Come along and count with me.
    There are seven days, you see.
    Sunday, Monday, Tuesday too,
    Wednesday, Thursday—just for you.
    Friday, Saturday—that's the end.
    Now let's sing it all again.
- Play Days of the Week to reinforce the sequence of the days of the week. Slap your knees, and clap your hands in rhythm as you say the days. Have children participate in this activity.

Following Assessment 4, Part B—Actions

- Play What Am I Touching? charades using pictures of body parts (wrist, chin, elbow, knees, hair, and so on). Place the pictures facedown on a table, and have a child pick one (without showing it to the other children). The child then touches the body part, and the other children guess. The child who responds correctly can say the whole thing and act out the next picture.
- Have a grab bag of illustrated actions. A child picks one and performs the action. The child then says, "I am _____." The class responds with "You are _____." Finally, everyone performs the action and says, "We are _____."
- Play Simon Says, exaggerating the use of pronouns. For example, "Simon says touch **your** eyes." This can be used to reteach both the names of body parts and the use of pronouns.

Following Assessment 4, Part C—Part/Whole

- Assign children to groups to make Silly Faces. Ask one child to draw an outline of a face. Each child adds another part to the face (Expanded Language Activities for lessons 31–35, page vi).
- Given puzzles of faces with parts, have children work the puzzles. As each face piece is put into place, the child says the whole thing, such as "A head has eyes."
- Assign each child a partner. Have children take turns drawing each other's faces. Collect the drawings, and have the entire class identify the faces (Expanded Language Activities, Lessons 36–40, page vii).

Activities for Additional Support

Following Assessment 4, Part D—Prepositions

- Direct four or five children to stand or sit in different areas of the classroom while the rest of the group identifies who is where using the terms *on, in front of,* and *over* (Expanded Language Activities for lessons 31–35, page vi).
- Read the story "Marvin the Eagle," emphasizing the prepositions *on, over,* and *in front of.* Have children respond to questions about the story (Presentation Book A, Storybook 1, page 24).

Following Assessment 4, Part E—Opposites

- Using real objects or pictures of objects and their opposite pairs—*full/not full, wet/not wet,* and *big/not big*—have children identify which object goes with which part of the opposite pair.
- Using pictures of objects on a bingo card and the opposite pairs—*full/not full, wet/not wet,* and *big/not big*—have children play a bingo game.

Enrichment Activities

At Mastery
Children who score at or above 90 percent

Following Assessment 4, Part A—Information

- Have children make predictions about the weather for today and for tomorrow using the names of the days of the week (Expanded Language Activities for lessons 36–40, page vii).
- Using a teacher-made large calendar, have children draw pictures of one activity they completed for each day of the week and say the name of the day.

Following Assessment 4, Part B—Actions

- Play Spin a Person (Language Activity Masters Book 1, lesson 35).
- Use the Roll the Cube! Actions Block, allowing each child several turns to roll the cube and perform an action. After performing each action, the child says, "I am _____." The class responds with "You are _____." Finally, everyone performs the action and says, "We are _____" (Language Activity Masters Book 1, lesson 10).

Following Assessment 4, Part C—Part/Whole

- Have children make Silly Faces by cutting out parts of different faces from magazines (Expanded Language Activities for lessons 31–35, page vi).
- Give children pictures of faces with parts missing, and have them identify each part that is missing.
- Use the How Tall Am I? Giraffe Chart (Language Activity Masters Book 2, lesson 40).

Following Assessment 4, Part D—Prepositions

- Read the story "Marvin the Eagle," emphasizing the prepositions *on, over,* and *in front of.* Have children respond to questions about the story and say the whole thing (Presentation Book A, Storybook 1, page 24).
- Play Preposition Hunt by giving children clues about where something is in the classroom. Include the prepositions *on, over,* or *in front of* (Picture Cards User's Guide, page 11).

Following Assessment 4, Part E—Opposites

- Using the opposite pairs—*full/not full, wet/not wet,* and *big/not big*—have children develop a bulletin board with illustrations of opposites.
- Play Meet Your Object Match using opposite pairs. Have two sets of picture cards of objects children have learned. Give each child one card. Explain that each card has a match and that they need to find the child who is holding the match. Ask each matched pair to stand together and hold up their cards.

Tips for Teachers

English Language Learners

- See Extra Help guidelines for children who score below 90 percent or groups that average below 80 percent on Assessment 4.
- See Expanded Language Activities on pages vi and vii in Presentation Book A.
- Continue labeling classroom objects in English and, when available, in children's native languages.
- Describe and model mouth formations for words in "Say it slowly; say it fast" activities; then guide children while practicing with a mirror.
- Show realia or other visuals of objects and concepts.
- Use Total Physical Response (TPR) to show concepts of pronouns by saying a word or phrase and then demonstrating the concept by pantomiming or gesturing. For example, say, "The book is in front of me," and then hold book in front of you. Guide children as they use TPR to demonstrate the concept.
- At the end of the day, review the day's activities by asking what the class did first, next, and last.
- Take a vocabulary walk around the school or neighborhood, and ask children to identify known objects. Ask children to point to things they don't know the name of, and ask if anyone else knows the name. Have all children repeat the name of the object.
- Have children add to their picture dictionaries by cutting out pictures from magazines or newspapers. Then play the You Be the Teacher game by having children take turns being the teacher and asking others, "What does _____ mean?"
- Use primary language equivalents when available, and then ask children to say the words in English.

Home Connections

- Encourage children to share their completed workbook pages with their families.
- Provide an audiotape to use with picture flash cards of common objects, actions, and concepts taught (for example, on and over).
- Encourage children to practice mouth formations with a mirror at home.
- Encourage parents to help children identify realia and other visuals of common objects at home.
- Encourage parents to incorporate "Say it slowly; say it fast" activities throughout the day. Encourage children to practice with a mirror at home as needed.
- Encourage parents to play the What's Missing? game at home.
- Encourage parents to ask children their town, city, or area name.
- Encourage parents to help children practice using primary language equivalents and English words when possible.
- Encourage parents to read to their children or tell them a story using the pictures from the book, asking them questions about the story. Encourage children to respond in complete sentences.
- Encourage parents to continue adding words their child is having difficulty with to his or her Word Wall.

Approaching Mastery

Children who score below 90 percent or groups that average below 80 percent

Following Assessment 5, Part A—Information

- Using a teacher-made large calendar, have children draw pictures of one activity they completed for each day of the week and state the name of the day.
- Divide children into two groups. Group one says the first day of the week, and then group two says the next day. Continue until all the days of the week have been named. Practice in different ways, such as with a slow voice, fast voice, quiet voice, and loud voice.
- Sing the song "Today Is" to the tune of "Mary Had a Little Lamb." Change the word in the blank to match the day of the week.

    Today is _____, _____, _____.
    Today is _____; let's all sing a song.
    It will be a fun day, fun day, fun day.
    It will be a fun day all day long.
    Sing a song of _____, _____, _____.
    Sing a song of _____ all day long.

Following Assessment 5, Part B—Actions

- Play Spin a Person (Language Activity Masters Book 1, lesson 35).
- Using the Actions Picture Cards, have children identify the action and then say the whole thing using the appropriate pronoun (Picture Cards 1 through 9).
- Use Mr. Owl Puppet and Finger Play (Language Activity Masters Book 2, lesson 45).

Following Assessment 5, Part C—Opposites

- Play Opposites Concentration. This can be played by pairs of children. Make pairs of matching opposite cards or pictures. Divide the cards or pictures into two stacks with matching cards in the opposite stack. Turn the stacks facedown. Let each child turn one card or picture over from each set. If the pair matches, he or she says the name of the opposite pair and keeps the set. The other child gets the next turn.
- Bring into the classroom object pairs that represent the opposite pairs that have been taught (*full/not full, wet/not wet, big/not big, long/not long*). Have children identify each of the object pairs, answer questions about the pair, and say the whole thing about the pair.

Following Assessment 5, Part D—Prepositions

- Read the poem "Painting," and then ask children questions about where the paint and objects are located, using the prepositions *on, over,* or *in front of* (Presentation Book A, Storybook 1, page 13).
- Using objects previously taught, have children place the object *on, over,* or *in front of* another object and then say the whole thing about where the object is. For example, using a pencil, the child places it *on the table, over the table,* or *in front of the table.*

Following Assessment 5, Part E—Part/Whole

- Using the Objects Picture Cards, have children identify the whole object and each part. Then have children say the whole thing (Picture Cards 17, 87, 95, 132, 159, 160, and 200).
- Using real objects taught in lessons 28 through 49, have children stand beside or hold the object (head, table, pencil, toothbrush, wagon, and tree). As you name the parts of each object, children touch each part. Then touch each part while children name the part and say the whole thing.
- Read and act out the following Action Poem with children:

    This is a circle that is my head. (Make a large circle with both hands.)
    This is my mouth with which words are said. (Point to your mouth.)
    These are my eyes with which I see. (Point to your eyes.)
    This is my nose that's part of me. (Point to your nose.)
    This is the hair that grows on my head, (Point to your hair.)
    And this is my hat all round and red. (Place your hands on your head with your fingers pointing up and touching.)

Enrichment Activities

At Mastery

Children who score at or above 90 percent

Following Assessment 5, Part A—Information

- Use the Roll the Cube! Actions Block. Change the pictures to reflect the days of the week, school, city, seven, teacher, and a child. Allow each child to roll the cube, then repeat the word-name that is appropriate for the picture (Language Activity Master Book 1, lesson 10).
- Have children make a Days of the Week picture book.

Following Assessment 5, Part B—Actions

- Read "Oscar the Worm," and have children identify characters throughout the story, say what each character is doing, and then say the whole thing about what the characters are doing (Presentation Book A, Storybook 1, page 14).
- Assist children in developing their own picture book, using actions. As children discuss the book, have them respond to questions by saying the whole thing and using action words and pronouns.
- Use Mr. Owl Puppet and Finger Play (Language Activity Masters Book 2, lesson 45).

Following Assessment 5, Part C—Opposites

- Have children make an Opposites Bulletin Board. They collect or draw pictures of opposite pairs and add them to the board as they learn new opposites.
- Cut pictures of opposite pairs from books, papers, or magazines. Glue or tape each pair into an Opposites Notebook that each child keeps.

Following Assessment 5, Part D—Prepositions

- Play Frog on a Log (Language Activity Masters Book 2, lesson 50).
- Play Prepositions—I Spy by giving children clues about where something is in the classroom. Include the prepositions *on, over,* and *in front of.*

Following Assessment 5, Part E—Part/Whole

- Play Build an Elephant (Language Activity Masters Book 1, lesson 45).
- Have children build their own object (table, pencil, toothbrush, wagon, tree, or elephant) using cores of paper towels and toilet paper rolls. Then have children explain the parts of the object as well as the name of the whole object (Expanded Language Activities for lessons 41–45, page vii).
- Play Spin a Person (Language Activity Masters Book 1, lesson 35).

Tips for Teachers

English Language Learners

- See Extra Help guidelines for children who score below 90 percent or groups that average below 80 percent on Assessment 5.
- See Expanded Language Activities on page vii in Presentation Book A.
- Continue labeling classroom objects in English and, when available, in children's native languages.
- Describe and model mouth formations for words in "Say it slowly; say it fast" activities, and then guide children while practicing with a mirror.
- Show realia or other visuals of objects and concepts.
- Use Total Physical Response (TPR) to model concepts by saying a word or phrase and then demonstrating the concept by pantomiming or gesturing. Guide children as they use TPR to demonstrate the concept.
- At the end of day, review the day's activities by asking what children did first, next, and last.
- Have children add to their picture dictionaries by cutting out pictures from magazines or newspapers. Then play the You Be the Teacher game by having children take turns being the teacher and asking others, "What does _____ mean?"
- Have children cut out pictures from magazines or newspapers and paste them in an order that tells a story. Children tell a story by stating what happened first, next, and last.
- Use primary language equivalents when available, and then ask children to say the words in English.

Home Connections

- Encourage children to share their completed workbook pages with their families.
- Provide an audiotape to use with picture flash cards of common objects, actions, and concepts taught.
- Provide a page of words for children to take home to practice "Sound it out; say it fast."
- Encourage children to practice mouth formations with a mirror at home.
- Encourage parents to help children identify realia and other visuals of common objects at home.
- Encourage parents to take their children on a vocabulary walk around the neighborhood and ask them to identify known objects. Ask children to point to things they don't know the names of. Parents can say the name and have children repeat it.
- Encourage parents to play the What's Missing? game at home.
- Encourage parents to ask children their town, city, or area name.
- Encourage parents to help children practice using primary language equivalents and English words when possible.
- Encourage parents to read to their children or tell them a story using the pictures from the book, asking them what happened first, next, and last.
- Encourage parents to continue adding words their child is having difficulty with to his or her Word Wall. Then have parents take words their child has learned off the Word Wall.

Assessment 6 (Lessons 51–60)

Approaching Mastery

Children who score below 90 percent or groups that average below 80 percent

Activities for Additional Support

Following Assessment 6, Part A—Information

- Use the Roll the Cube! Actions Block. Change the pictures to reflect the days of the week, school, city, seven, teacher, and a child. Allow each child to roll the cube and then repeat the word-name that is appropriate for the picture (Language Activity Masters Book 1, lesson 10).
- Have children make a Days of the Week picture book.

Following Assessment 6, Part B—Classification

- Using vehicles, have children name the type of vehicle and then say the whole thing about the vehicle.
- Have children cut out pictures of vehicles from magazines and advertisements and paste them onto construction paper to make a vehicle collage. Have each child describe their pictures to the class, making sure they say the whole thing and the rule about vehicles.

Following Assessment 6, Part C—Plurals

- Play Simon Says, and have children touch various body parts. Emphasize both singular and plural by having them touch a hand, both hands, an eye, eyes, an ear, ears, and so on. Then have children say the whole thing about what they are touching.
- Play a matching game where children match pictures of one object with a picture of multiple objects of the same type. For example, match a picture of one hand with a picture of two hands.

Following Assessment 6, Part D—Tense

- Using My Turtle from Language Activity Masters Book 1, lesson 60, have children make the turtle, complete the poem, and respond to questions about where the head of the turtle *is* and where the head of the turtle *was*.
- Place objects children have learned (such as a pencil, a cup, a glass, a piece of paper, a book, a chair, and an eraser) around the classroom where they can be seen. Ask a child to go to an object, tell the class where the object *is*, bring the object to you, and then tell the class where the object *was*. Play the game until every child has had an opportunity to find an object.

Following Assessment 6, Part E—Concept Application

- Read the story "Curious Carla Gets into Trouble," and have children respond to questions about the story (Presentation Book B, Storybook 2, page 8).
- Review the song "Five Green and Speckled Frogs." Have children sing the song and respond to questions about it (Language Activity Masters Book 2, lesson 50).

Enrichment Activities

At Mastery

Children who score at or above 90 percent

Following Assessment 6, Part A—Information

- Have children practice saying the days of the week. Each day, talk about what day it is and what you and the children do on that day. Using the pictures drawn on the teacher-made calendar from Assessment 4, have children choose one day and develop a class story about that day. Write the story for children on a large chart.
- Make a Day of the Week puzzle. Using the pictures drawn on the teacher-made calendar from Assessment 4, help children make a puzzle. Cut the pictures into large pieces, and then put them back together on a sheet of paper (Language Activity Masters Book 1, School–Home Link Newsletter 11).

Following Assessment 6, Part B—Classification

- Using the Vehicle Picture Cards (cards 187–200), have children name the type of vehicle and then say the whole thing about the vehicle.
- Have children cut out pictures of vehicles from magazines and advertisements, then paste them onto one-half of a sheet of construction paper. Then have children cut out pictures of things that are not vehicles and paste them on the other half. Have children describe their pictures to the class, making sure they say the whole thing and the rule about vehicles. If children would like, let them identify the objects that are not vehicles.
- Say the name of a place where you could go, and allow children to tell you how to get there— by bike, car, plane, or boat.

Following Assessment 6, Part C—Plurals

- Play tic-tac-toe. Make a game board with familiar pictures of singular and plural objects. Call out the pictures one at a time. Have children say the name of the object, using the singular or plural form appropriately, and have them place a counter on the game board. The first child to cover the pictures in a row wins. Clear the game board, and play several times.
- Play Concentration using the cards from Language Activity Masters Book 1, lesson 5. Make an additional set of cards with the plural of each object on them. Have children play the game and match the singular and plural cards.

Following Assessment 6, Part D—Tense

- Using any Picture Cards that have been taught, play Preposition Hunt, and ask questions that include the words *on, in, where is,* and *where was* (Picture Cards User's Guide, page 11).
- Read the story "Melissa Hides the Bag of Popcorn," and ask children questions which include the words *on, in, where is,* and *where was* (Presentation Book B, Storybook 2, page 1).

Following Assessment 6, Part E—Concept Application

- Read the story "Curious Carla Gets into Trouble." Ask children questions about the story, and have them make predictions about what will happen (Presentation Book B, Storybook 2, page 8).
- Read the story "Melissa Hides the Bag of Popcorn." Ask children questions about the story, and have them make predictions about what will happen (Presentation Book B, Storybook 2, page 1).

Tips for Teachers

English Language Learners

- See Extra Help guidelines for children who score below 90 percent or groups that average below 80 percent on Assessment 6.
- See Expanded Language Activities on page v in Presentation Book B.
- Continue labeling classroom objects in English and, when available, in children's native languages.
- Reinforce concepts of singular and plural by showing realia or other visuals of single and multiple objects.
- Use TPR to model concepts by saying a word or phrase and then demonstrating the concept by pantomiming or gesturing. Guide children as they use TPR to demonstrate the concept.

- Reinforce verb tenses by using the Action Grab Bag with pictures of actions. Children take turns pulling pictures of actions out of the bag and demonstrating actions. They tell what other children are doing while actions are being performed. After actions cease, children tell what actions were performed.
- Have children add to their picture dictionaries by cutting out pictures from magazines or newspapers. Then play the You Be the Teacher game by having children take turns being the teacher and asking others, "What does _____ mean?"
- Make a vehicle classification poster by having children cut out pictures of different vehicles from magazines or newspapers.
- Use primary language equivalents when available, and then ask children to say the words in English.

Home Connections

- Encourage children to share their completed workbook pages with their families.
- Provide an audiotape to use with picture flash cards of common objects, actions, and concepts taught.
- Provide a page of words for children to take home to practice "Sound it out; say it fast."
- Encourage children to practice mouth formations with a mirror at home.
- Encourage parents to help children understand concepts of singular and plural by identifying single and multiple objects at home.
- Encourage parents to help children identify and sort objects by color (for example, orange, green, and brown).
- Encourage parents to help children practice using primary language equivalents and English words when possible.
- Encourage parents to read to their children or tell them a story using the pictures from the book, asking them questions about the story. Encourage children to respond in complete sentences.
- Encourage parents to continue adding words their child is having difficulty with to his or her Word Wall. Then have parents take words their child has learned off the Word Wall.

Assessment 7 (Lessons 61–70)	Activities for Additional Support
Approaching Mastery Children who score below 90 percent or groups that average below 80 percent	**Following Assessment 7, Part A—Part/Whole** • Use A Portrait (Language Activity Masters Book 2, lesson 55). • Using the Picture Cards 17, 87, 95, 96, 132, 156, 157, 159, 160, 192, and 200, have children choose a card, identify each part, and then name the whole. Play several times, allowing each child to work with more than one card. • Use the Friendship Tree (Language Activity Masters Book 2, lesson 65). **Following Assessment 7, Part B—And—Actions** • Play Simon Says using single and sequenced multiple actions. Then have children say the whole thing about what they are doing (Picture Cards User's Guide, page 17). • Sing "If You're Happy and You Know It" to reinforce And—Actions: *If you're happy and you know it, clap your hands!* (Clap two times.) *If you're happy and you know it, clap your hands!* (Clap two times.) *If you're happy and you know it, your face will surely show it.* *If you're happy and you know it, clap your hands!* (Clap two times.) Repeat the song using "stomp your feet," "tap your head," "jump up and down," "clap your hands and stomp your feet," and "clap your hands and tap your head." Add other combinations as desired (a version of Expanded Language Activities for lessons 46–50, page vii).

Activities for Additional Support

Following Assessment 7, Part C—Tense
- Name an action, and have one child perform the action. Ask the other children to state what the child *is doing.* Ask the child to stop the action, and allow the other children to state what the child *was doing.* Play this several times using various actions, allowing each child to perform a few actions for the class.
- Using common classroom objects that children have learned (such as a ball, a clock, a crayon, a pencil, an eraser, a book, and a ruler), have children say where the object *is.* Then move the object; have children say where the object *was* and say the whole thing. Allow children several opportunities to respond to a variety of objects.

Following Assessment 7, Part D—Classification
- Play Vehicle Lotto (Language Activity Masters Book 1, lesson 70).
- Use My Kitchen (Language Activity Masters Book 2, lesson 70).

Following Assessment 7, Part E—Information
- Talk about what day it is today. Say "Today is _____, so what day will tomorrow be?" Talk about activities each child did today. Then ask each child to draw a picture of an activity that will happen tomorrow and tell the class about it (Language Activity Masters, School-Home Link Newsletter 13).
- Using a large calendar and pictures, have children describe and draw or cut out pictures to represent the following: today's weather, lunch menu, school activity schedule, tomorrow's weather, lunch menu, and school activity schedule. If time permits, have children develop their own personal calendars with the same information.

Following Assessment 7, Part F—Concept Application
- Read the story "Curious Carla Makes Everybody Happy." Have children respond to *why* questions about the story (Presentation Book B, Storybook 2, page 23).
- Teach children Getting Hotter . . . Getting Colder. Have one child face the wall while another child points to an object in the classroom. Then tell the first child to turn around. The other children give clues for locating the object by shouting "getting hotter" or "getting colder" to direct the child to the target object (Expanded Language Activities for lessons 51–55, page v).

Enrichment Activities

At Mastery

Children who score at or above 90 percent

Following Assessment 7, Part A—Part/Whole
- Use Elephant Mask (Language Activity Masters Book 2, lesson 60).
- Have children play Engine on the Track finger play to reinforce Part/Whole concepts:
  Here is the engine on the track. (Hold up thumb.)
  Here is the coal car, just in back. (Hold up pointer finger.)
  Here is the box car to carry freight. (Hold up middle finger.)
  Here is the mail car. Don't be late! (Hold up ring finger.)
  Way back here at the end of the train (Hold up little finger.)
  Rides the caboose through the sun and rain. (Move hand as if a train were moving.)

Following Assessment 7, Part B—And—Actions
- Have children make Action Booklets by pasting or drawing action pictures of people and animals onto folded paper. Allow children to tell the class what the people and animals are doing. Encourage children to have the action characters complete more than one action, and ask them to say the whole thing about what the characters are doing (Expanded Language Activities for lessons 61–65, page v).
- Using the grab bag of illustrated actions from lessons 26–30, allow children to choose two and perform the actions. The rest of the class tells what the child is doing by saying the whole thing (Expanded Language Activities for lessons 26–30, page vi).

Following Assessment 7, Part C—Tense
- Using the Actions Picture Cards (Cards 1–9), hold up one card, and ask children what the person *is doing.* Next, put the card down, and ask children what the person *was doing.* Have children respond with both the action and by saying the whole thing about what the person *is* or *was* doing. Have children play several times, allowing each child to respond to more than one picture card (a version of Act it Out! from the Picture Cards User's Guide, page 7).

Enrichment Activities

- Using common classroom objects that children have learned such as a ball, a clock, a crayon, a pencil, an eraser, a book, and a ruler, have each child choose an object and say where the object *is*. Then have the child move the object and say where the object *was* by saying the whole thing. Allow children several opportunities to respond to a variety of objects.

Following Assessment 7, Part D—Classification

- Have children begin a Classification Scrapbook. Have them cut out and paste (or draw) pictures of vehicles and food onto construction paper. As they learn new classifications, allow children to add to their scrapbooks.

Following Assessment 7, Part E—Information

- Play a game similar to My Grandmother's Trunk. Children sit in a circle. Begin the game with a silly sentence that includes a day of the week; for example, say, "Monday, my pet dragon ate a ball." The next child repeats the sentence and adds another sentence describing what happened the day before or the day after. Each child in the group adds a sentence which includes the name of a day of the week (a version of Expanded Language Activities for lessons 21–25, page vi).
- Have children keep a picture diary of what they do each day for one week. Allow children to share their diaries with the class.

Following Assessment 7, Part F—Concept Application

- Read the poem "What We Saw" to children. Have children respond to each of the questions in the poem (Presentation Book B, Storybook 2, page 19).
- Read the story "Curious Carla Makes Everybody Happy." Have children respond to "why" questions and role-play the story (Presentation Book B, Storybook 2, page 23).
- Teach children to play the game What Am I Thinking Of? Start by giving them one piece of information. For example, say, "I am thinking of something in this classroom. What am I thinking of?" Call on three children. If no one answers correctly, give another piece of information. For example, say, "You use this to write with." Then call on three different children. Continue this pattern until children have given the correct answer (Expanded Language Activities for lessons 61–65, page v).

Tips for Teachers

English Language Learners

- See Extra Help guidelines for children who score below 90 percent or groups that average below 80 percent on Assessment 7.
- See Expanded Language Activities on page v in Presentation Book B.
- Continue labeling classroom objects in English and, when available, in children's native languages.
- Show realia or other visuals of objects and concepts.
- Use TPR to model concepts by saying a word or phrase and then demonstrating the concept by pantomiming or gesturing. Guide children as they use TPR to demonstrate the concept.
- Make a food classification poster by having children cut out pictures of different foods from magazines or newspapers.
- Group objects in the classroom by what material they are made of. For example, have children gather objects made of plastic, paper, or cloth.
- Take a vocabulary walk around the school or neighborhood. Ask children to identify triangular shapes and circular shapes.
- Have children add to their picture dictionaries by cutting out pictures from magazines or newspapers. Then play the You Be the Teacher game by having children take turns being the teacher and asking others "What does _____ mean?"
- Use primary language equivalents when available, and then ask children to say the words in English.

Home Connections

- Encourage children to share their completed workbook pages with their families.
- Provide an audiotape to use with picture flash cards of common objects, actions, and concepts taught.
- Provide a page of words for children to take home to practice "Sound it out; say it fast."
- Encourage children to practice mouth formations with a mirror at home.
- Encourage parents to help children identify objects made of various materials (for example, plastic, paper, or cloth) at home.
- Encourage parents to help children identify triangular shapes and circular shapes at home.
- Encourage parents to help children practice using primary language equivalents and English words when possible.
- Encourage parents to read to their children or tell them a story using the pictures from the book, asking them what happened first, next, and last.
- Encourage parents to continue adding words their child is having difficulty with to his or her Word Wall. Then have parents take words their child has learned off the Word Wall.

Assessment 8 (Lessons 71–80)

Activities for Additional Support

Approaching Mastery

Children who score below 90 percent or groups that average below 80 percent

Following Assessment 8, Part A—Information

- Using the Picture Cards 134, 135, 137, 138, and 141, play Where Do I Work? (Picture Cards User's Guide, page 11).
- Have each child choose one of the following people: a dentist, farmer, storekeeper, firefighter, or teacher. Have the child pretend to be that person and describe what they do and where they do it. Allow them to draw a picture of themselves as that person at work.

Following Assessment 8, Part B—Tense

- Teach children the finger play Where Is Thumbkin? Ask children questions using *is* and *was*. Then allow children to respond using the correct tense and saying the whole thing (Expanded Language Activities for lessons 66–70, page v).
- Using the Action Booklets children made previously, have each child tell what the animals and people *are doing* and *were doing.* Then have children say the whole thing (Expanded Language Activities for lessons 61–65, page v).

Following Assessment 8, Part C—Classification

- Bring into class play objects from the following classifications: food, containers, vehicles, and clothing. Have children separate each object into the correct classification and then name the object. Have children say the whole thing about the classification and the name of the object.
- Using Picture Cards 98–110 (Containers); 111–123 (Food); 187–200 (Vehicles); 39, 41–45, 47–48 (Clothing), play What Doesn't Belong? (Picture Cards User's Guide, page 12).

Following Assessment 8, Part D—Plurals

- Read aloud *The Three Billy Goats Gruff.* Emphasize the words *up, under,* and *over* (Expanded Language Activities for lessons 76–80, page vi).
- Use Over and Under the Bridge (Language Activity Masters Book 2, lesson 75).
- Read the story "Dozy at the Zoo," emphasizing the prepositions in bold print. Allow children to respond to the questions in the story (Presentation Book B, Storybook 2, page 31).
- Play One or More? Fooler Game. Tell children you are going to try to fool them by saying a body part that means one or more than one. Children must touch the part or parts. Make sure that children touch both parts if you say the plural. Use leg/legs, wrist/wrists, eye/eyes, tooth/teeth, finger/fingers, foot/feet, elbow/elbows, ear/ears, and arm/arms (Language Activity Masters Book 1, School-Home Link Newsletter 15).

Following Assessment 8, Part E—Part/Whole

- Using Picture Cards 17, 87, 95, 96, 132, 156, 157, 159, 160, 192, and 200, have children identify the whole picture and then the parts.

Activities for Additional Support

- Use puzzles of the following items: head, table, pencil, toothbrush, elephant, wagon, tree, umbrella, car, flower, and coat. Have children name the parts of each item and then the whole as they work the puzzle.
- Use the Criss-Cross Mobile. Talk about the parts of the mobile (Language Activity Masters Book 1, lesson 75).

Following Assessment 8, Part F—Concept Application
- Use My Kitchen (Language Activity Masters Book 2, lesson 70).
- Tell children the rule "If you can eat it, it's food." Have children repeat the rule several times. Then show pictures of food and non-food items one at a time. After each item, children should say "food" or "non-food" (Language Activity Masters Book 1, School-Home Link Newsletter 14).

Enrichment Activities

At Mastery

Children who score at or above 90 percent

Following Assessment 8, Part A—Information
- Play the guessing game What Am I Thinking Of? using the terms dentist, city, farm, store, sky, sun, clouds, firefighter, and teacher (Expanded Language Activities for lessons 71–75, page vi).
- Build a model of your city or town using play objects that can be labeled as a dentist and office, vehicles children have learned, a farm, animals children have learned, a store, trees, grass, water, a firefighter and fire engine, and a school with children and a teacher. Allow children to play together with the model, having them say the whole thing as they play.

Following Assessment 8, Part B—Tense
- Prepare a grab bag of illustrated actions. A child picks up an illustration and performs the action. The other children identify the action and tell what the child *is doing* and *was doing.* Allow each child the opportunity to perform an action (Expanded Language Activities for lessons 81–85, page vi).
- Play Sequence a Story. Use three or four pictures to help children recall what *is* happening and what *was* happening. First tell a story using three or four pictures to emphasize important details. Then arrange the pictures out of sequence in front of the group. Finally, rearrange the pictures in order with the help of children. Then ask what *is* happening and what *was* happening.

Following Assessment 8, Part C—Classification
- Play Two, Three, or Four Corners using the Picture Cards from the vehicles, food, containers, and clothing classes (Picture Cards User's Guide, page 12).
- Have children cut out and paste (or draw) pictures of food onto construction paper. Allow children to add these pages to their Classification Scrapbook (Expanded Language Activities for lessons 76–80, page vi).

Following Assessment 8, Part D—Plurals
- Read aloud *The Three Billy Goats Gruff.* Emphasize the words *up, under,* and *over.* Have children make stick puppets to role-play the story (Expanded Language Activities for lessons 76–80, page vi).
- Read the story "Dozy at the Zoo," emphasizing the prepositions in bold print. Allow children to respond to the questions in the story. Have children act out parts of Dozy's dream (Presentation Book B, Storybook 2, page 31).
- Play One or More? Fooler Game. Tell children you are going to try to fool them by saying a body part that means one or more than one. Children must touch the part or parts. Make sure that children touch both parts if you say the plural. Use *leg/legs, wrist/wrists, eye/eyes, tooth/teeth, finger/fingers, foot/feet, elbow/elbows, ear/ears,* and *arm/arms* (Language Activity Masters Book 1, School-Home Link Newsletter 15).

Following Assessment 8, Part E—Part/Whole
- Use pictures of a head, a table, a pencil, a toothbrush, an elephant, a wagon, a tree, an umbrella, a car, a flower, and a coat. Have children cut the pictures into pieces that show the parts of each item. Then allow children to make their own puzzles with the pieces (Expanded Language Activities for lessons 81–85, page vi).

Enrichment Activities

- Have children draw pictures of the following items with the parts on the wrong objects: head, table, pencil, toothbrush, elephant, wagon, tree, umbrella, car, flower, and coat. After children have finished their pictures, allow them to share their pictures and explain what is wrong.

Following Assessment 8, Part F—Concept Application

- Read the poem "What Did I Do?" Have children respond to the questions within each verse (Presentation Book B, Storybook 2, page 28).
- Tell children the rule "If you can eat it, it's food." Have children repeat the rule several times. Then name food and non-food items one at a time. After each item, children should say "food" or "non-food" (Language Activity Masters Book 1, School-Home Link Newsletter 14).

Tips for Teachers

English Language Learners

- See Extra Help guidelines for children who score below 90 percent or groups that average below 80 percent on Assessment 8.
- See Expanded Language Activities on page vi in Presentation Book B.
- Continue labeling classroom objects in English and, when available, in children's native languages.
- Show realia or other visuals of objects and concepts.
- Use TPR to model concepts by saying a word or phrase and then demonstrating the concept by pantomiming or gesturing. Guide children as they use TPR to demonstrate the concept.
- Make a classification poster for containers and clothing by having children cut out pictures of different containers and clothing from magazines or newspapers.
- Have children add to their picture dictionaries by cutting out pictures from magazines or newspapers. Then play the You Be the Teacher game by having children take turns being the teacher and asking others "What does _____ mean?"
- Use primary language equivalents when available, and then ask children to say the words in English.

Home Connections

- Encourage children to share their completed workbook pages with their families.
- Provide an audiotape to use with picture flash cards of common objects, actions, and concepts taught.
- Provide a page of words for children to take home to practice "Sound it out; say it fast."
- Encourage children to practice mouth formations with a mirror at home.
- Encourage parents to help children identify objects made of various materials (for example, glass or wood) at home.
- Encourage parents to help children practice using primary language equivalents and English words when possible.
- Encourage parents to read to their children or tell them a story using the pictures from the book, asking them questions about the story. Encourage children to respond in complete sentences.
- Encourage parents to continue adding words their child is having difficulty with to his or her Word Wall. Then have parents take words their child has learned off the Word Wall.

Activities for Additional Support

Approaching Mastery

Children who score below 90 percent or groups that average below 80 percent

Following Assessment 9, Part A—Information
- Use the Weather Wheel (Language Activity Masters Book 2, lesson 80).
- Use Who Am I Going to See? Forest Puzzle (Language Activity Masters Book 2, lesson 85).

Following Assessment 9, Part B—Materials
- Use These Boots Were Made for Walking (Language Activity Masters Book 1, lesson 90).
- Go on a class treasure hunt for objects made of the following materials: cloth, paper, plastic, leather, glass, wood, metal, and concrete. As children find the objects, have them identify the object, what it is made of, and say the whole thing about the object.

Following Assessment 9, Part C—Actions—Tense
- Read "Melissa Will Try," emphasizing the verb tense and allowing children to respond to questions in the story (Presentation Book B, Storybook 2, page 42).
- Play Simon Says using the following terms: on, over, in front of, in, in back of, under, next to, and between. As children perform each action ask them to say where their _____ *is*. After they have performed each action ask children to say where their _____ *was*.

Following Assessment 9, Part D—Opposites
- Use Short to Long Doggie (Language Activity Masters Book 1, lesson 55).
- Use play objects with opposite pairs including *full/empty, big/small, wet/dry, long/short,* and *old/young.* Mix up the objects, and have children match each pair. After each pair has been matched, have children say sentences about the matches.
- Have children draw one half of any opposite pair of their choice on one side of a piece of paper that has been folded in half. Have them draw the other half of the opposite pair on the other side of the paper. For example, a child might draw a small dog on the left and a big dog on the right. Then have children describe their pictures to the class.

Following Assessment 9, Part E—Classification
- Use Fill Up the Refrigerator! (Language Activity Masters Book 1, lesson 85).
- Use On the Move Matching (Language Activity Masters Book 2, lesson 90).
- Read "Dozy Gets A Vehicle," and have children respond to the questions about the story and identify the different classifications of objects (Presentation Book C, Storybook 3, page 1).
- Read "My Dream," and have children respond to the questions about the poem, identify the different classifications of objects, and draw a picture of what they dream of becoming when they grow up (Presentation Book C, Storybook 3, page 7).

Following Assessment 9, Part F—Concept Application
- Play Take Away. Find some containers such as a basket, a box, a bag, a jar, and a bowl. Put them on a table along with classroom objects that are not containers, such as a towel, a toy, a book, a crayon, a pencil, a ruler, and a piece of paper. Say this rule: "If you can put something in it, it's a container." Ask children to identify and say the whole thing about the containers. Also have them identify the other objects as not containers and say the whole thing.
- Play Frog on a Log (Language Activity Masters Book 2, lesson 50).

Enrichment Activities

At Mastery

Children who score at or above 90 percent

Following Assessment 9, Part A—Information
- Play Where Do I Work? In this game, children match workers to their work locations. Select several cards which children have been taught, such as a school, a fire station, a doctor's office, a grocery store, and a farm. Lay the cards faceup on a table. Give a description of a worker, and ask children to name where the worker works. After they have provided the answer, children can turn that card over (Picture Cards User's Guide, page 11).
- Have children develop a picture newspaper. The newspaper could include school and community information, pictures and names of children in the class, a weather section, and an events calendar.

Enrichment Activities

Following Assessment 9, Part B—Materials

- Play the Blindfold game. Collect small objects made from various materials, and place them in a large paper bag. Some examples might be a plastic toy, a juice glass, a leather billfold, a metal fork, a sock, and a piece of paper. Blindfold one child and have the child pull an object from the bag, feel it, and guess what material the object is made of. Repeat the process with each child in the group. When all children have had an opportunity to participate, let the class look at and discuss the objects and the materials from which they were made.
- Have children cut pictures from magazines or draw objects made of one of the following materials: cloth, paper, plastic, leather, glass, wood, metal, and concrete. Have each child make a Material Scrapbook and then share his or her scrapbook with the class. Have children say the whole thing about the object and the materials from which they are made. Each child may have a different material.

Following Assessment 9, Part C—Actions—Tense

- Play an action game based upon what children are wearing. Children are to follow your verbal directions. For example, all boys wearing something with stripes will put one hand in front of one knee; all girls wearing something red will clap in back of their heads; all children wearing jeans will put one finger between their eyes. Different children tell what they *are doing* and what they *were doing* using the prepositional phrases correctly (a version of Expanded Language Activities for lessons 86–90, page v).
- Read "Melissa Will Try," emphasizing the verb tense and allowing children to respond to questions in the story. Afterward, allow children to role-play the story (Presentation Book B, Storybook 2, page 42).

Following Assessment 9, Part D—Opposites

- Show children pictures depicting the following opposite pairs: *full/empty, big/small, wet/dry, long/short,* and *old/young.* Have children generate sentences using the opposites, such as "The elephant is big" or "The monkey is small."
- Play Opposites Concentration using cards that represent the opposite pairs children have learned (a version of Object Concentration in Language Activity Masters Book 1, lesson 5).

Following Assessment 9, Part E—Classification

- Read "Dozy Gets a Vehicle," having children respond to the questions about the story, identify the different classifications of objects, and role-play the characters (Presentation Book C, Storybook 3, page 1).
- Read "My Dream," and have children respond to the questions about the poem, identify the different classifications of objects, and draw a picture of what they dream of becoming when they grow up (Presentation Book C, Storybook 3, page 7).

Following Assessment 9, Part F—Concept Application

- Play Thumbs Up: Where Am I Hiding? Pre-select Animal Picture Cards that children have learned, and lay those cards on a table. Give children verbal clues to an animal, and allow children to use the clues to identify the animal you are thinking about. When children know the animal, they give a thumbs-up (Picture Cards User's Guide, page 15).
- Play a version of What's Missing? by using several Picture Cards that children have learned. Have one child be the player and spread out the cards. Then ask the other children to close their eyes. The player will then hide two or three of the cards. When the player says "ready," the other children may open their eyes. The other children ask questions to determine which pictures are missing. The player answers with "yes" or "no" and shows the missing pictures as they are identified. Play until all children have had an opportunity to be the player (Picture Cards User's Guide, page 10).

Tips for Teachers

English Language Learners

- See Extra Help guidelines for children who score below 90 percent or groups that average below 80 percent on Assessment 9.
- See Expanded Language Activities on page vi in Presentation Book B and page v in Presentation Book C.
- Continue labeling classroom objects in English and, when available, in children's native languages.
- Show realia or other visuals of objects and concepts.
- Use TPR to model concepts by saying a word or phrase and then demonstrating the concept by pantomiming or gesturing. Guide children as they use TPR to demonstrate the concept.
- Take a vocabulary walk around the school or neighborhood. Ask children to identify rectangular shapes.
- Make an animal classification poster by having children cut out pictures of different animals from magazines or newspapers.
- Have children add to their picture dictionaries by cutting out pictures from magazines or newspapers. Then play the You Be the Teacher game by having children take turns being the teacher and asking others "What does _____ mean?"
- Use primary language equivalents when available, and then ask children to say the words in English.

Home Connections

- Encourage children to share their completed workbook pages with their families.
- Provide an audiotape to use with picture flash cards of common objects, actions, and concepts taught.
- Provide a page of words for children to take home to practice "Sound it out; say it fast."
- Encourage children to practice mouth formations with a mirror at home.
- Encourage parents to help children identify objects made of various materials (for example, metal or leather) at home.
- Encourage parents to help children identify rectangular shapes at home.
- Encourage parents to help children practice using primary language equivalents and English words when possible.
- Encourage parents to read to their children or tell them a story using the pictures from the book, asking them what happened first, next, and last.
- Encourage parents to continue adding words their child is having difficulty with to his or her Word Wall. Then have parents take words their child has learned off the Word Wall.

Assessment 10 (Lessons 91–100)	**Activities for Additional Support**

Approaching Mastery

Children who score below 90 percent or groups that average below 80 percent

Following Assessment 10, Part A—Information

- Have each child repeat his or her address and telephone number to you.
- Collect some small objects made of various materials previously discussed (cloth, paper, plastic, leather, glass, wood, metal, and concrete). Choose a child to be "it." Blindfold the child, and put an object on the table. Ask the child to feel the object and guess what it is made of. After the child has guessed the object, remove the blindfold, and allow the child to see if his or her guess was correct. Repeat the game with each child in the group.

Following Assessment 10, Part B—Part/Whole—Body Parts

- Use Build a House (Language Activity Masters Book 1, lesson 95).
- Use A Portrait, and replace the person's whole body instead of just a head. Allow children to identify such additional body parts as eyebrows, elbows, neck, knees, hands, feet, arms, legs, and hips (Language Activity Masters Book 2, lesson 55).

Activities for Additional Support

Following Assessment 10, Part C—Tense

- Reread the story "Oscar the Worm." Have children respond to questions about where the animals *are* and where the animals *were* (a version of Expanded Language Activities for lessons 96-100, page v).
- Play Teddy Bear Actions. Have children perform various actions. After each action, ask children, "What *are* you doing?" and "What *were* you doing?" Alter the actions to create a new poem: for example, *Touch your nose, the floor, your knees,* and *sit down.*

  Teddy bear, teddy bear, turn around.
  Teddy bear, teddy bear, touch the ground.
  Teddy bear, teddy bear, tie your shoes.
  Teddy bear, teddy bear, that will do!

Following Assessment 10, Part D—Some/All

- Play Listen and Do! Tape-record simple directions that include the use of *some/all*. Have the group follow the directions with real objects. Leave time on the tape for the group to perform each action and say the whole thing about what they are doing.
- Play Missing Objects. Place several objects on a table. Have children close their eyes and remove either *some* or *all* of the objects. When children open their eyes, they tell whether *some* or *all* of the objects are missing. Then they say the whole thing about the objects. Allow different children to come to the table and be the teacher who removes the objects.

Following Assessment 10, Part E—Same

- Use small objects from the categories vehicles, people, and animals. Mix the objects, and then allow children to separate them into the appropriate category. When children have finished separating the objects, have them state how they are the *same*. For example, they might say "These objects are the *same* because they are all vehicles." Play the game several times with different objects, allowing each child an opportunity to play and state how the objects are the *same*.
- Divide children into groups of three or four. Give each group four or five pictures of objects from the same class such as vehicles, food, or containers. Have each group tell the other children how the objects are the *same* and say the whole thing about what is the same.

Following Assessment 10, Part F—Concept Application

- Use the Friendship Tree (Language Activity Masters Book 2, lesson 65).
- Read the story "Melissa on the Ranch," and have children respond to questions about the story. Have children respond by saying the whole thing (Presentation Book C, Storybook 3, page 9).

Enrichment Activities

At Mastery

Children who score at or above 90 percent

Following Assessment 10, Part A—Information

- Read aloud *The Three Little Pigs.* Talk about the kinds of materials the pigs used to build their houses and why some were stronger than others. Have children identify the building materials shown in the pictures.
- Play a memory game with children to help review the materials from which objects are made. Tell children to look around the classroom and identify as many objects as possible made of cloth. Ask children to name the cloth objects. Then have children close their eyes without peeking and tell you the names of objects they can remember that are made of cloth. Repeat the game with paper, plastic, leather, glass, wood, metal, and concrete.

Following Assessment 10, Part B—Part/Whole—Body Parts

- Use Spin a Person, and add a discussion of such body parts as elbows, neck, knees, hands, feet, arms, legs, and hips (Language Activity Masters Book 1, lesson 35).
- Make a picture of each child by tracing his or her outline onto a large piece of butcher paper. Have children identify body parts that have been taught and color in the outlines. When all the outlines are finished, hang up the pictures. Have children identify and describe each picture (a version of Expanded Language Activities for lessons 11–15, page v).

Enrichment Activities

Following Assessment 10, Part C—Tense

- Children role-play the story "Oscar the Worm." Have children respond to questions about where the animals *are* and where the animals *were*. Assign children to be Oscar, the lion, the elephant, the bird, and the narrator. The narrator tells each part of the story as children role-play their parts (Expanded Language Activities for lessons 96–100, page v).
- Play Line Up. Pick three children to stand in a line in front of the group. Allow the remaining children to say where each of the three children *is* and where all three *are*. After children have looked at the standing children for a few seconds, have children cover their eyes. Then rearrange the order of the standing children. Have the group open their eyes and see who can tell where each of the three children *was* and where all three *were*. Play the game until all children have had the opportunity to be part of the group of three.

Following Assessment 10, Part D—Some/All

- Put an assortment of small toys or objects on a table. Use a towel or scarf to cover up *some* or *all* of the objects. Ask children to tell what you have covered using a complete sentence. Play several times until each child has had an opportunity to respond.
- Play May I Have It? Pick one child to be "It." Give "It" several of the same small object (such as cotton balls, cotton swabs, pencils, erasers, crayons, paper clips, and so on) to give to the other children in the group. Each of the children asks "It" to give him or her *some* or *all* of the objects. When the object(s) have been given, the child says the whole thing about what he or she has, using the appropriate *some/all* word. If the child says the whole thing correctly, he or she gets to be "It." Play the game until all children have had the opportunity to be "It" and the opportunity to receive the objects.

Following Assessment 10, Part E—Same

- Play an action game based upon what children are wearing. Children are to follow your verbal directions. For example, all boys wearing the *same* color shirt will wave; all girls with the *same* color hair will clap two times. Have individual children tell what is the *same*, and then say the whole thing about what is the same.
- Use Picture Cards from the categories vehicles, people, and animals. Mix the cards. Then, allow children to separate the cards into the appropriate category. When children have finished separating the cards, have them state how they are the *same*. For example, they might say "These cards are the *same* because they are all vehicles." Play the game several times with different cards, allowing each child an opportunity to play and state how the cards are the *same*.

Following Assessment 10, Part F—Concept Application

- Read "Dozy Gets a Vehicle" again. Have children respond to questions about the story. Focus on the rule "If it can take you places, it's a vehicle." Before you ask children questions, repeat the rule, and then have them repeat the rule.
- Read "Denise Builds a House." Have children respond to questions about the story (Presentation Book C, Storybook 3, page 17).

Tips for Teachers

English Language Learners

- See Extra Help guidelines for children who score below 90 percent or groups that average below 80 percent on Assessment 10.
- See Expanded Language Activities on page v in Presentation Book C.
- Continue labeling classroom objects in English and, when available, in children's native languages.
- Reinforce the months of the year by making a birthday wall to show in what months children's birthdays occur.
- Reinforce the concept of *same* by talking about children who share the same birthday month.
- Show realia or other visuals of objects and concepts
- Use TPR to model concepts by saying a word or phrase and then demonstrating the concept by pantomiming or gesturing. Guide children as they use TPR to demonstrate the concept.
- Take a vocabulary walk around the school or neighborhood. Ask children to identify objects made of concrete.

- Make a farm animal classification poster by having children cut out pictures of different animals that can be found on a farm from magazines or newspapers.
- Have children add to their picture dictionaries by cutting out pictures from magazines or newspapers. Then play the You Be the Teacher game by having children take turns being the teacher and asking others "What does _____ mean?"
- Use primary language equivalents when available, and then ask children to say the words in English.

Home Connections

- Encourage children to share their completed workbook pages with their families.
- Provide an audiotape to use with picture flash cards of common objects, actions, and concepts taught.
- Provide a page of words for children to take home to practice "Sound it out; say it fast."
- Encourage children to practice mouth formations with a mirror at home.
- Encourage parents to help children identify the birthday months of family members.
- Encourage parents to help children practice using primary language equivalents and English words when possible.
- Encourage parents to read to their children or tell them a story using the pictures from the book, asking them questions about the story. Encourage children to respond in complete sentences.
- Encourage parents to continue adding words their child is having difficulty with to his or her Word Wall. Then have parents take words their child has learned off the Word Wall.

Assessment 11 (Lessons 101–110)

Activities for Additional Support

Approaching Mastery

Children who score below 90 percent or groups that average below 80 percent

Following Assessment 11, Part A—Information
- Use Red Light–Green Light (Language Activity Masters Book 1, lesson 80).
- Use Squirrel, Squirrel, Where's Your Nut? to reinforce common information (Language Activity Masters Book 2, lesson 100).

Following Assessment 11, Part B—Actions—First/Next/After
- Use Over and Under the Bridge to reinforce *first/next/after* (Language Activity Masters Book 2, lesson 75).
- Use Simon Says Animal Hands to reinforce *first/next/after* (Language Activity Masters Book 2, lesson 105).

Following Assessment 11, Part C—Same
- Using the Tools, Furniture, Containers, Food, Clothing, and Buildings Picture Cards, play What Doesn't Belong? (Picture Cards User's Guide, page 12).
- Use Going Places (Language Activity Masters Book 1, lesson 110).

Following Assessment 11, Part D—Part/Whole
- Use Build a House (Language Activity Masters Book 1, lesson 95).
- Use the Elephant Mask (Language Activity Masters Book 2, lesson 60).
- Reread "Denise Builds a House." Have children respond to questions about the parts of the house and say the whole thing about the parts (Presentation Book C, Storybook 3, page 17).

Following Assessment 11, Part E—Opposites
- Use the Short to Long Doggie (Language Activity Masters Book 1, lesson 55).
- Use the Weather Wheel to reinforce the opposites *wet/dry* (Language Activity Masters Book 2, lesson 80).

Activities for Additional Support

Following Assessment 11, Part F—Classification/Same

- Have children cut out a picture of a food item, an article of clothing, and an animal from magazines and glue them onto separate pieces of paper. Paste each picture onto a separate piece of freezer paper. Each display shows one class children have learned (a version of Expanded Language Activities for lessons 91–95, page v).
- Have children make Classification notebooks. They first find pictures of objects from each class they have learned—vehicles, animals, containers, plants, and clothing. Children paste the pictures into notebooks that have dividers for the different classes. They will add to their notebooks as they learn new classes (Expanded Language Activities for lessons 106–110, page v).

Following Assessment 11, Part G—Concept Application

- Read the poem "My Balloon," and allow children to respond to questions about the poem (Presentation Book C, Storybook 3, page 26).
- Read the story "Doris Goes to the Store," and allow children to respond to questions about the story (Presentation Book C, Storybook 3, page 23).

Enrichment Activities

At Mastery

Children who score at or above 90 percent

Following Assessment 11, Part A—Information

- Have children draw pictures of something they did each month of the year (possibly associated with an American holiday). Individual children recite "In January I . . . ." As they tell what they did, they hold up a picture showing what they did (a version of Expanded Language Activities for lessons 106–110, page v).
- Have children start Common Information notebooks. They draw pictures and cut out magazine pictures that illustrate the places and people they are learning about (Expanded Language Activities for lessons 101–105, page v).

Following Assessment 11, Part B—Actions—First/Next/After

- Read the story "Melissa on the Ranch," and have children respond to first/next/after questions about the story. Have children respond by saying the whole thing. Finally, allow children to role-play what Melissa did first, next, and after in the story (Presentation Book C, Storybook 3, page 9).
- Read aloud Goldilocks and the Three Bears. Have them tell you where Goldilocks goes first, next, and after. Allow children to role-play the story, emphasizing the order of events. Give each child a piece of paper that has three boxes on it labeled first, next, and after. Have children draw pictures of what happens in the story in the appropriate box.

Following Assessment 11, Part C—Same

- Use Going Places (Language Activity Masters Book 1, lesson 110).
- Use Vehicles Picture Cards, and play Vehicles: Land, Water, Clouds? Add "What does this vehicle do?" to the questions already asked in the activity (Picture Cards User's Guide, page 7).
- Using the Animals Picture Cards, play Animal Sort Call Outs, emphasizing categories that are the same (Picture Cards User's Guide, page 13).

Following Assessment 11, Part D—Part/Whole

- Use Build a House (Language Activity Masters Book 1, lesson 95).
- Reread "Denise Builds a House." Have children respond to questions about the parts of the house, role-play the story, and say the whole thing about the parts (Presentation Book C, Storybook 3, page 17).
- Using play blocks, allow children to follow the steps Denise follows in building a house. Then allow children to follow the steps Dad follows in fixing the house (Presentation Book C, Storybook 3, page 17).

Following Assessment 11, Part E—Opposites

- Use The Lion and the Mouse Pop Up to reinforce the opposites big/small (Language Activity Masters Book 2, lesson 95).

Enrichment Activities

- Play I Am Thinking of . . . , a guessing game about opposites within the classroom. Give children clues about opposite pairs (full/empty, big/small, wet/dry, long/short, and tall/short) you have placed in various places in the classroom. Continue giving clues until every child has an opportunity to find one of the opposite pairs.

Following Assessment 11, Part F—Classification/Same

- Each child draws a picture of a food item, an article of clothing, and an animal on separate pieces of paper. Paste all pictures onto three large pieces of butcher paper. Each display shows one class children have learned (Expanded Language Activities for lessons 91–95, page v).
- Have children make Classification notebooks. They first find pictures of objects from each class they have learned—vehicles, animals, containers, plants, and clothing. Children paste the pictures into notebooks that have dividers for the different classes. They will add to their notebooks as they learn new classes (Expanded Language Activities for lessons 106–110, page v).
- Divide children into groups of three or four. Give each group four or five pictures of objects from the same class—for example, vehicles, food, or containers. Have each group tell the other children what its class is (Expanded Language Activities for lessons 96–100, page v).

Following Assessment 11, Part G—Concept Application

- Read the poem "My Balloon," and allow children to respond to questions about the poem (Presentation Book C, Storybook 3, page 26).
- Read the story "Doris Goes to the Store." Allow children to respond to questions and role-play the story (Presentation Book C, Storybook 3, page 23).

Tips for Teachers

English Language Learners

- See Extra Help guidelines for children who score below 90 percent or groups that average below 80 percent on Assessment 11.
- See Expanded Language Activities on page v in Presentation Book C.
- Continue labeling classroom objects in English and, when available, in children's native languages.
- Show realia or other visuals of objects and concepts.
- Use TPR to model concepts by saying a word or phrase and then demonstrating the concept by pantomiming or gesturing. Guide children as they use TPR to demonstrate the concept.
- Reinforce the concepts of *before, during,* and *after* by having children discuss what they do before, during, and after school.
- Take a vocabulary walk around the school or neighborhood. Ask children to identify square shapes.
- Make a building classification poster by having children cut out pictures of different buildings from magazines or newspapers.
- Have children add to their picture dictionaries by cutting out pictures from magazines or newspapers. Then play the You Be the Teacher game by having children take turns being the teacher and asking others "What does _____ mean?"
- Encourage children to use new words at home. The next day, ask, "Did anyone share the words at home?"
- Use primary language equivalents when available, and then ask children to say the words in English.

Home Connections

- Encourage children to share their completed workbook pages with their families.
- Provide an audiotape to use with picture flash cards of common objects, actions, and concepts taught.
- Provide a page of words for children to take home to practice "Sound it out; say it fast."

Home Connections

- Encourage children to practice mouth formations with a mirror at home.
- Encourage parents to help children identify objects at home made of rubber.
- Encourage parents to help children identify square shapes at home.
- Encourage parents to help children practice using primary language equivalents and English words when possible.
- Encourage parents to read to their children or tell them a story using the pictures from the book, asking them what happened first, next, and last.
- Encourage parents to continue adding words their child is having difficulty with to his or her Word Wall. Then have parents take words their child has learned off the Word Wall.

Activities for Additional Support

Approaching Mastery

Children who score below 90 percent or groups that average below 80 percent

Following Assessment 12, Part A—Information

- Sing "This Month Is" to the tune of "Mary Had a Little Lamb," inserting the names of the months in the blank spaces.

    This month is _____, _____, _____.
    This month is _____; let's sing a song.
    It will be a fun month, fun month, fun month.
    It will be a fun month all month long.
    Sing a song of _____, _____, _____.
    Sing a song of _____ all month long.

- Sing the song "Count the Days" to the tune of "Twinkle, Twinkle, Little Star."

    Come along and count with me.
    There are seven days, you see.
    Sunday, Monday, Tuesday too,
    Wednesday, Thursday—just for you.
    Friday, Saturday—that's the end.
    Now let's sing it all again!

Following Assessment 12, Part B—Action—Some/All/None

- Put an assortment of small toys or objects on a table. Use a towel or scarf to cover up *some, all,* or *none* of the objects. Ask children to tell what you have covered, using a complete sentence. Play several times until each child has had an opportunity to respond.
- Play Simon says using actions that can be completed with the words *all, some,* or *none.* Allow children to take turns being Simon.

Following Assessment 12, Part C—Classification

- Play Meet Your Class Match. Have two sets of picture cards of the same classifications children have learned. Give each child one card. Explain that each card has a match and that the child needs to find the person who is holding the card that matches. Ask each matched pair to stand together, hold up their cards, and say the whole thing about their card and its classification.
- Using classifications such as vehicles, food, containers, clothing, animals, and buildings, choose a class, and give children several examples in that class. Then ask each child to tell you another. For example, say, "Truck, car, taxi. Tell me another." (Bus, train, and plane are some possible choices.) Make sure that children give different examples rather than the same or just a few examples. Play until each child has had an opportunity to respond to several classifications.

Activities for Additional Support

Following Assessment 12, Part D—Before/After

- Play Sequence a Story by using three or four pictures to help children recall what happens *before* and *after.* Follow these steps:
    1. Tell a story using three or four pictures to emphasize the important details.
    2. Arrange the pictures out of sequence in front of the group.
    3. Ask what happens *before* and *after* in the story. Ask the group to rearrange the pictures. (This also can be done to review *first/next/after.*)
- Use Follow the Leader (Language Activity Masters Book 1, lesson 115).
- Have children follow the steps of a simple recipe. Talk about what happens *before* and *after* as children make the recipe. Afterward, allow children to eat what they have made.

Following Assessment 12, Part E—Concept Application

- Read "Dozy Paints the House." Have children respond to questions about the story (Presentation Book C, Storybook 3, page 35).
- Have children role-play the story "Marvin the Eagle." Assign children to play the parts of Marvin, Marvin's brother, the cow, and one or more narrators. The narrators tell the parts of the story as the characters role-play them (Expanded Language Activities for lessons 111–115, page v).

Enrichment Activities

At Mastery

Children who score at or above 90 percent

Following Assessment 12, Part A—Information

- Use the Carpenter with Tools (Language Activity Masters Book 1, lesson 100).
- Use Whose Hat? Match and Mix Booklet (Language Activity Masters Book 2, lesson 120).

Following Assessment 12, Part B—Action—Some/All/None

- Play Word Series by presenting a series of words to the group (things in the classroom, things we wear, food we eat, animals, colors, and so on). Ask each child in the group to repeat either *all, some,* or *none* of the words. Play the game until each child has had the opportunity to respond to *all, some,* and *none.* Here are some examples:
    Table, chair, flag
    Fish, monkey, bird
    Shoe, hat, shirt
- Using just the action pictures from BLM 115 B, have children color *all, some,* or *none* of the pictures in each row. Then go back and have children do the actions shown in the pictures they have colored (Language Activity Masters Book 1, lesson 115).

Following Assessment 12, Part C—Classification

- Use Mail a Letter (Language Activity Masters Book 1, lesson 105).
- Use the Whale's Ocean Wheel (Language Activity Masters Book 2, lesson 110).

Following Assessment 12, Part D—Before/After

- Help children send a letter to a friend or parent. Ask each child to draw a picture. Have the child put the picture in an envelope. Talk about what must be done *before* and *after* putting the envelope in a mailbox. Show children how to write the address and put on the stamp. Talk about how the envelope will get to their friends or parents.
- Assign each child, or small group of children, a chore or task within the classroom to complete. Use the words *before* and *after* when describing the chore or task. Have children repeat the directions. After they have finished the chore or task, have children draw pictures showing what they did and the order in which the steps of the chore or task were completed.
- Have children follow the steps of a simple recipe. Talk about what happens *before* and *after* as children make the recipe. Afterward, allow children to eat what they have made.

Following Assessment 12, Part E—Concept Application

- Play Thumbs Up: Where Am I Hiding? using the Animals and Locations Picture Cards (Picture Cards User's Guide, page 15).
- Play the Where Do I Live? Sorting Activity using the Animals, Buildings, and Locations Picture Cards (Picture Cards User's Guide, page 11).
- Read "Dozy Paints the House." Have children respond to questions about the story and role-play the story (Presentation Book C, Storybook 3, page 35).

Tips for Teachers

English Language Learners

- See Extra Help guidelines for children who score below 90 percent or groups that average below 80 percent on Assessment 12.
- See Expanded Language Activities on page v in Presentation Book C.
- Continue labeling classroom objects in English and, when available, in children's native languages.
- Show realia or other visuals of objects and concepts.
- Use TPR to model concepts by saying a word or phrase and then demonstrating the concept by pantomiming or gesturing. Guide children as they use TPR to demonstrate the concept.
- Make a plant classification poster by having children cut out pictures of different plants from magazines or newspapers.
- Have children add to their picture dictionaries by cutting out pictures from magazines or newspapers. Then play the You Be the Teacher game by having children take turns being the teacher and asking others "What does _____ mean?"
- Use primary language equivalents when available, and then ask children to say the words in English.

Home Connections

- Encourage children to share their completed workbook pages with their families.
- Provide an audiotape to use with picture flash cards of common objects, actions, and concepts taught.
- Provide a page of words for children to take home to practice "Sound it out; say it fast."
- Encourage children to practice mouth formations with a mirror at home.
- Encourage parents to help children identify objects by color (for example, pink and purple) at home.
- Encourage parents to help children practice using primary language equivalents and English words when possible.
- Encourage parents to read to their children or tell them a story using the pictures from the book, asking them questions about the story. Encourage children to respond in complete sentences.
- Encourage parents to continue adding words their child is having difficulty with to his or her Word Wall. Then have parents take words their child has learned off the Word Wall.

Assessment 13 (Lessons 121–130)

Activities for Additional Support

Approaching Mastery

Children who score below 90 percent or groups that average below 80 percent

Following Assessment 13, Part A—Information

- Read *The Year at Maple Hill Farm* by Alice and Martin Provensen. Have children look for picture clues that help them identify the seasons of the year. Then have children say the whole thing about the season.
- Play What Will You Wear? Lay an assortment of Seasons and Clothing Picture Cards on the table to play the game. Sing the following rhyme to the tune of "Mary Had a Little Lamb," and insert a child's name and a season.

    _____ (name), what will you wear?
    Will you wear?
    Will you wear?
    _____ (name), what will you wear?
    Wear in the _____ (season)?

Have children take turns picking up a Clothing card and placing it next to the correct Season card. Each child tells what he or she will wear in what season (Picture Card User's Guide, page 9).

Activities for Additional Support

Following Assessment 13, Part B—Opposites
- Play Let's Go Fishing, an opposites activity (Language Activity Masters Book 2, lesson 115).
- Use Cover Up! (Language Activity Masters Book 1, lesson 120).

Following Assessment 13, Part C—Common Information
- Play Find the Shapes and Beat the Timer! For each round of the game, use up to all four Shapes Picture Cards. Set out two to four cards, and tell children that when it is their turn, they have to find and touch items with this shape and return to their seat before the timer goes off. For each child, change the cards and set the timer for one minute. Then children say, "Ready, set, find the shapes!" Provide help as needed so children can find the items with the specified shape before the timer goes off. After children have found items, have them say the whole thing about the shape and the object (Picture Cards User's Guide, page 17).
- Sing "Old MacDonald Had a Farm" with children to practice some of the farm animal names and sounds. After singing, have children identify the various animals from the song that might be found on a farm. Finally, have children draw a picture of a farm with the animals mentioned in the song. Sing the song repeatedly with the following animals and noises: horse–neigh, pig–oink, sheep–baa, chicken–cluck, duck–quack, dog–arf, and cat–meow.

Following Assessment 13, Part D—Where, Who, When, What
- Read *The Little Red Hen* to children. Have them respond to *where, who, when,* and *what* questions about the story.
- Read a familiar story such as *Henny Penny* or *The Gingerbread Man*. Have children say the repeated lines of the story with you. Then have them respond to *where, who, when,* and *what* questions about the story (Expanded Language Activities for lessons 121–125, page v).

Following Assessment 13, Part E—Classification
- Use Animal Babies on the Farm (Language Activities Master Book 1, lesson 130).
- Play the following finger play with children:
  Homes
  This is a nest for Mr. Bluebird.
  (*Cup both hands together.*)
  This is a hive for Mrs. Bee.
  (*Put fists together to form a hive.*)
  This is a hole for bunny rabbit.
  (*Hold fingers loosely in a circle.*)
  And this is a house for me.
  (*Put fingertips together to form a roof.*)

Following Assessment 13, Part F—Same/Different
- Using a variety of play vehicles, animals, clothing, and containers, have each child choose an object and tell the class how the object is the same and how it is different from other objects.
- Using Picture Cards of items familiar to the children, ask children how the two items are the same and how they are different. Some items to use include a basket and a bowl, a desk and a dresser, and a truck and a train.

Enrichment Activities

At Mastery

Children who score at or above 90 percent

Following Assessment 13, Part A—Information
- Read *The Ox-Cart Man* by Donald Hall. Have children look for picture clues that help them identify the seasons of the year. Then have children say the whole thing about the season.
- Using a twelve-month calendar, have children draw pictures on each month to indicate in what season of the year that month comes. For months that include the changing of a season, allow children to draw one picture for each season. Hang the calendars on a season bulletin board.

Following Assessment 13, Part B—Opposites
- Use The Rule of the Striped Door (Language Activity Masters Book 2, lesson 125).
- Use Happy/Sad Puppet (Language Activity Masters Book 1, lesson 125).

Enrichment Activities

At Mastery
 	
Children who score at or above 90 percent
	Following Assessment 13, Part C—Common Information
	
	• Play Where Do I Work? Have children match workers to their work locations. Select several Picture Cards from Locations and Buildings, such as a school, a fire station, a doctor's office, a grocery store, and a farm. Lay the cards faceup on the table. Give a description of a worker, and ask children to name the location or building where the person works. After children have identified a location or building, they can turn that card over (Picture Cards User's Guide, page 11).
	• Read *Walking Through the Jungle* by Julie Lacome. As children listen to the story, have them identify the different things in a jungle and say the whole thing. Then have children draw their own pictures of a jungle.
	
	Following Assessment 13, Part D—Where, Who, When, What
	
	• Have children role-play "Dozy Gets a Vehicle." Use pictures of the different things that Dozy is supposed to bring. A narrator tells the story. The other children in the group can say the repeated lines in the story. Then have children respond to *where, who, when,* and *what* questions about the story (Expanded Language Activities for lessons 126–130, page iv).
	• Have children "build a story." Cut out three to five pictures of people from a magazine, three to five pictures of places, and three to five pictures of activities.
	  1. Have children explain what each picture shows.
	  2. Have children "build a story" by picking one picture from each group (people, places, and activities).
	  3. Allow children to tell a story by telling about the person, what is happening, and where it is happening.
	Repeat the procedures until all children have had an opportunity to tell a different story.
	
	Following Assessment 13, Part E—Classification
	
	• Show children some hand tools such as a hammer, screwdriver, pliers, saw, paintbrush, and drill. Talk about how each tool can be used. Give children examples of jobs, and ask which tool would be used for each job. For example, ask, "Which tool would you use to . . .
	    put a picture on a wall (hammer and nail),
	    make a hole for a door in a bird house (drill),
	    cut a board in two (saw),
	    change the color of a wall (paintbrush),
	    tighten a loose screw (screwdriver), or
	    get a tight lid off a jar (pliers)?"
	• Play a word game with children. Say, "I am going to name some things that are in the same class. You are going to tell me the class." Name two things in any of the following classes: clothing, vehicles, food, animals, or buildings. For example, say, "A coat and a sock." Children respond with "Clothing." Repeat the game until all children have had the opportunity to name in which class two objects belong.
	
	Following Assessment 13, Part F—Same/Different
	
	• Ask children how two things are the same and how they are different. Some words to use include a fish and a boat, a bird and an airplane, and a horse and a car.
	• Using the Animal Flip Book, have children complete the book, color the animals, and then tell how each animal is the same and how it is different. Allow each child the opportunity to say one same and one different statement (Language Activity Masters Book 1, lesson 65).

Tips for Teachers

English Language Learners	• See Extra Help guidelines for children who score below 90 percent or groups that average below 80 percent on Assessment 13.
	• See Expanded Language Activities on page v in Presentation Book D.
	• Continue labeling classroom objects in English and, when available, in children's native languages.
	• Show realia or other visuals of objects and concepts.
	• Use TPR to model concepts by saying a word or phrase and then demonstrating the concept by pantomiming or gesturing. Guide children as they use TPR to demonstrate the concept.
	• Reinforce the concept of *when* by having children tell when they do everyday activities. For example, ask, "Do you eat dinner before or after school?"
	• Take a vocabulary walk around the school or neighborhood. Ask children to identify things made of brick.
	• Have children cut out pictures from magazines or newspapers that show *who, what, where,* and *when.* Have children paste the pictures on construction paper and share their stories.
	• Make a tool classification poster by having children cut out pictures of different tools from magazines or newspapers.
	• Have children identify which months are in each season. Identify the essential features of the seasons.
	• Have children add to their picture dictionaries by cutting out pictures from magazines or newspapers. Then play the You Be the Teacher game by having children take turns being the teacher and asking others "What does _____ mean?"
	• Use primary language equivalents when available, and then ask children to say the words in English.

Home Connections

• Encourage children to share their completed workbook pages with their families.

• Provide an audiotape to use with picture flash cards of common objects, actions, and concepts taught.

• Provide a page of words for children to take home to practice "Sound it out; say it fast."

• Encourage children to practice mouth formations with a mirror at home.

• Encourage parents to help children identify in what season each family member's birthday occurs.

• Encourage parents to help children identify tools used at home.

• Encourage parents to help children practice using primary language equivalents and English words when possible.

• Encourage parents to read to their children or tell them a story using the pictures from the book, asking them what happened first, next, and last.

• Encourage parents to continue adding words their child is having difficulty with to his or her Word Wall. Then have parents take words their child has learned off the Word Wall.

Activities for Additional Support

Approaching Mastery

Children who score below 90 percent or groups that average below 80 percent

Following Assessment 14, Part A—Information

- Use Shop Till You Drop! (Language Activity Masters Book 1, lesson 135).
- Use Occupation Concentration (Language Activity Masters Book, lesson 140).

Following Assessment 14, Part B—Same/Different

- Play Odd One Out! using the Clothing and Animals Picture Cards. Choose three cards from one category and one card from the other category—belt, hat, shirt, and cat, for example. Have four children stand up, and give them each a card to hold and show to the group. After the seated children have had a few moments to look at the cards, ask, "On the count of three, who is the odd one out?" Children respond with, "Cat!" Ask, "Why did you say *cat?*" Try to elicit responses such as "Because a cat is an animal, and socks, hat, and a shirt are clothing." The person who was the "Odd One Out" can help select the next category to use for the next round (Picture Cards User's Guide, page 16).
- Have a box of common classroom objects. Have each child choose two objects from the box and tell the class how those two objects are the same and different. Play until each child has had at least one turn.

Following Assessment 14, Part C—Comparatives

- Put a variety of different-sized objects on a table. Use such things as a book, pencil, penny, plate, a big toy, or a small toy. Ask children to choose two objects and tell which is bigger or smaller. For example, a child might choose a penny and a cup and say, "The penny is smaller than the cup," or "The cup is bigger than the penny." Continue until all children have had an opportunity to compare objects.
- Play a word game with children. Say, "A roof is bigger than a door," or "A refrigerator is bigger than a spoon." Have children think of examples and take turns finishing sentences. For example, say, "A tree is bigger than _____." Children respond by naming things that are smaller such as a flower, a dog, or an apple. Play the game until each child has had an opportunity to think of at least one example and to finish as least one sentence.

Following Assessment 14, Part D—Where, Who, When, What

- Read "Dozy Goes Fishing." Have children respond to *where, who, when,* and *what* questions about the story (Presentation Book D, Storybook 4, page 1).
- Read "Dozy Goes on a Hike." Have children respond to *where, who, when,* and *what* questions about the story (Presentation Book D, Storybook 4, pages 9).

Following Assessment 14, Part E—Actions—Or

- Using the action pictures from Language Activity Masters Book 1, lesson 115, show children three pictures of what you are going to do. Have children choose those three pictures from their own set of picture cards. For example, tell children you are going to touch your knee **or** touch your head **or** clap your hands. Show them those three pictures. Ask children such questions as "What am I going to do?" or "Am I going to touch my knee?" or "Am I going to cover my eyes?" Complete one action such as touching your head. Have children choose the correct picture and hold it up. Make sure each child is holding the correct picture. Then ask such questions as "Did I touch my knee?" and "Did I touch my head?" Finally, have children say the whole thing about what you did.

Following Assessment 14, Part F—Absurdities

- Read "Denise Fixes the Inside of the House," having children respond to questions about the absurdities (Presentation Book D, Storybook 4, page 17).
- Give children examples, and ask them to tell you whether or not the example is absurd. Some examples include:
  NOT ABSURD
  "I talked to your parent on the phone today."
  "I saw a rabbit in the school playground today."
  ABSURD
  "I talked to a frog on the phone today."
  "I saw an elephant on the school playground today."

Activities for Additional Support

Following Assessment 14, Part G—Rules

- Have children play a position game. Seat children in a large circle. Draw a large rectangle on the floor. Each child is to have a toy animal or a picture of an animal. Show each animal, and have children identify the animal. Then give directions such as "All horses should be inside the rectangle; all cows should be next to the horses; all sheep should be outside the rectangle." Play until all children follow the directions correctly and are able to participate with an animal (Expanded Language Activities for lessons 131–135, page iv).
- Choose a rule from the Teacher's Guide, and have children draw a picture that represents the rule (*Language for Learning* Teacher's Guide).

Enrichment Activities

At Mastery

Children who score at or above 90 percent

Following Assessment 14, Part A—Information

- Divide the class into several groups. Assign each group one of the following locations: a farm, a city, an ocean, a forest, or a jungle. Have children in each group collect pictures about their location and paste them onto a mural. When the murals are finished, have each group tell about its mural, and hang the murals in the classroom (Expanded Language Activities for lessons 136–140, page iv).
- Play Line 'Em Up. Lay out four Seasons Picture Cards. Have children line up. Give a clue about a season, and have the first child say the season. If the season is correct, the child goes to the back of the line. If the season is not correct, the child sits down, and the next child in line gets to take a turn.
  Example clues:
  Leaves fall from the trees in the . . . <u>fall</u>.
  I like to go swimming on hot days in the . . . <u>summer</u>.
  I put on my hat and coat to keep warm in the . . . <u>winter</u>.
  (Picture Cards Users Guide, page 14)

Following Assessment 14, Part B—Same/Different

- Using the classification notebooks made after Assessment 11, have children add pictures of things that are both same and different. Have each child tell the class how the pictures are both same and different.
- Have children make a bulletin board of things that are the same and different. Divide the board into three categories: things that are the same on the left, things that are the same and different in the middle, and things that are different on the right. Children can cut pictures from magazines to place on the board. After the board is complete, discuss with children the pictures in each of the three categories. Note: Children will need your assistance to make sure that the same and different categories are correct.

Following Assessment 14, Part C—Comparatives

- Read *The Lion and the Mouse*. Have children discuss what is bigger and what is smaller in the fable.
- Read *Little Penguin* by Patrick Benson. Have children discuss what is bigger and what is smaller. Then allow children to draw pictures of bigger and smaller characters in the story.

Following Assessment 14, Part D—Where, Who, When, What

- Children role-play "Melissa Hides the Bag of Popcorn." Assign children to role-play the parts of Melissa, her sister, and the narrator. Children can say the repeated lines and respond to *where, who, when,* and *what* questions about the story (Expanded Language Activities for lessons 136–140, page v).
- Read "Dozy Goes Fishing." Have children role-play the story using a narrator, Dad, and Dozy. Then have children respond to *where, who, when,* and *what* questions about the story (Presentation Book D, Storybook 4, page 1).
- Read "Dozy Goes on a Hike." Have children role-play the story using a narrator, Dad, and Dozy. Then have children respond to *where, who, when,* and *what* questions about the story (Presentation Book D, Storybook 4, page 9).

Enrichment Activities

Following Assessment 14, Part E—Actions—Or

- Have children sit in a circle, and choose one child to be "It." Give "It" several directions to complete, using the format "_____ (child's name) is going to clap **or** snap **or** tap." Ask the class questions such as "What is _____ going to do?" and "Is _____ going to snap?" After children have responded to the questions, have "It" perform the action of his or her choice. Then ask children what "It" did, having them say the whole thing. Repeat the game with a variety of actions, allowing each child the opportunity to be "It."
- Using the vehicle lotto board from Language Activity Masters Book 1, lesson 70, tell children you are going to have them choose such items as a bike **or** a boat **or** a taxi. Ask such questions as "What am I going to choose?" and "Am I going to choose a boat?" and "Am I going to choose an airplane?" After children respond, choose one of the objects. Repeat the game several times.

Following Assessment 14, Part F—Absurdities

- Read the story "Denise Fixes the Inside of the House," having children role-play the story and respond to questions about the absurdities (Presentation Book D, Storybook 4, page 17).
- Make Absurd Pictures. Cut out pictures from magazines, and change them to be silly. For example, if children find a picture of a girl talking on the phone, cut out a picture of a shoe and paste it over the phone. Ask each child to explain why the new picture is absurd (Expanded Language Activities for lessons 146–150, page iv).

Following Assessment 14, Part G—Rules

- Choose a rule or rules from the Teacher's Guide, and have children draw a picture that represents the rule. Using the pictures that children have drawn, choose a picture, and ask questions about the picture that will help the other children identify the rule the picture illustrates. Play until each child's picture and all the rules have been used. This may occur over several days.
- Using a rule or rules from the Teacher's Guide, have children draw a picture that violates the rule and explain what part of the picture violates the rule.

Tips for Teachers

English Language Learners

- See Extra Help guidelines for children who score below 90 percent or groups that average below 80 percent on Assessment 14.
- See Expanded Language Activities on page iv in Presentation Book D.
- Continue labeling classroom objects in English and, when available, in children's native languages.
- Show realia or other visuals of obje cts and concepts.
- Use TPR to model concepts by saying a word or phrase and then demonstrating the concept by pantomiming or gesturing. Guide children as they use TPR to demonstrate the concept.
- Have children compare classroom objects by size. For example, the teacher's desk is bigger than the children's desks.
- Have children cut out pictures from magazines or newspapers that show *who, what, where,* and *when.* Have children paste pictures on construction paper and share their stories.
- Make a furniture classification poster by having children cut out pictures of different kinds of furniture from magazines or newspapers.
- Have children identify which months are in each season.
- Have children add to their picture dictionaries by cutting out pictures from magazines or newspapers. Then play the You Be the Teacher game by having children take turns being the teacher and asking others, "What does _____ mean?"
- Use primary language equivalents when available, and then ask children to say the words in English.

Home Connections

- Encourage children to share their completed workbook pages with their families.
- Provide an audiotape to use with picture flash cards of common objects, actions, and concepts taught.
- Provide a page of words for children to take home to practice "Sound it out; say it fast."
- Encourage children to practice mouth formations with a mirror at home.
- Encourage parents to help children identify types of furniture at home.
- Encourage parents to help children practice using primary language equivalents and English words when possible.
- Encourage parents to read to their children or tell them a story using the pictures from the book, asking them questions about the story. Encourage children to respond in complete sentences.
- Encourage parents to continue adding words their child is having difficulty with to his or her Word Wall. Then have parents take words their child has learned off the Word Wall.

**Assessment 15
(Lessons 141–150)**

Activities for Additional Support

Approaching Mastery

Children who score below 90 percent or groups that average below 80 percent

Following Assessment 15, Part A—Information

- Make seasons murals. Divide the class into four groups, and assign each group a season. Have children cut out magazine pictures or draw pictures appropriate to their season. Then have each group paste its pictures onto a large piece of paper to make a mural. Hang the murals in the classroom or in the hallways (Expanded Language Activities for lessons 141–145, page iv).
- Make a birthday calendar by using twelve large pieces of cardboard. Write the name of a month on each piece. Have children say the names of the months. Then ask each child to tell his or her birthday month. Group children according to the month of their birth. Give each group the cardboard labeled with their birth month, and have the group draw a picture of a birthday cake on the cardboard. After children complete the drawings, hang the birthday calendar on the wall (Expanded Language Activities for lessons 141–145, page iv).
- Use Animal Babies on the Farm (Language Activity Masters Book 1, lesson 130).

Following Assessment 15, Part B—Actions—Or

- Have children sit in a circle, and choose one child to be "It." Give "It" several directions to complete, using the format "_____ (child's name) is going to clap **or** snap **or** tap." Ask the class questions such as "What is _____ going to do?" and "Is _____ going to snap?" After children have responded to the questions, have "It" perform the action of his or her choice. Then ask children what "It" did, having them say the whole thing. Repeat the game with a variety of actions, allowing each child the opportunity to be "It."
- Using the vehicle lotto board from Language Activity Masters Book 1, lesson 70, tell children you are going to have them choose such items as a bike **or** a boat **or** a taxi. Ask such questions as "What am I going to choose?" and "Am I going to choose a boat?" and "Am I going to choose an airplane?" After children respond, choose one of the objects. Repeat the game several times.

Following Assessment 15, Part C—Materials

- Use the Mountain of Materials Game (Language Activity Masters Book 2, lesson 145).
- Choose Picture Cards from the Buildings, Clothing, Common Objects, Containers, Furniture, and Vehicles categories. Mix the cards up and turn them facedown. Have children choose a card and name the material the item is made of. Play several times so each child has an opportunity to participate (Picture Cards 30–48, 77–110, 124–132, and 187–200).

Following Assessment 15, Part D—Opposites

- Use The Rule of the Striped Door (Language Activity Masters Book 2, lesson 125).
- Use the Happy/Sad Puppet (Language Activity Masters Book 1, lesson 125).

Activities for Additional Support

Following Assessment 15, Part E—Absurdities

- Make Absurdity pictures. Have children draw pictures or cut out magazine pictures that convey absurd situations. Children paste them onto construction paper. Have each child describe why the picture is absurd. Label a bulletin board *Absurdities,* and put the pictures on it (Expanded Language Activities for lessons 146–150, page iv).
- Read *The Cat in the Hat,* by Dr. Seuss. Talk about what is absurd in the story.

Following Assessment 15, Part F—Rules

- Use Who Lives in the Ocean? (Language Activity Masters Book 2, lesson 140)
- Using the pictures children drew after Assessment 14 about a rule or rules from the Teacher's Guide, have them draw a picture that violates the rule and explain what part of the picture violates the rule.

Following Assessment 15, Part G—Same/Different

- Use Animal Babies on the Farm again. Have children describe the baby animals and tell how they are the same and different from the adult animals of the same breed (a version of Language Activity Masters Book 1, lesson 130).
- Read "Miss Edna Does the Same Thing," having children identify what Miss Edna does that is the same and what she does that is different (Presentation Book D, Storybook 4, page 37).

Following Assessment 15, Part H—Where, Who, When, What

- Make play clay and allow children to design "food." Have some children pretend to be customers and others pretend to be servers in a restaurant. After children have played for several minutes, ask them to respond to *where, who, when,* and *what* questions about their play.
- Read "Dozy Delivers the Nails." Have children respond to *where, who, when,* and *what* questions about the story (Presentation Book D, Storybook 4, page 25).

Enrichment Activities

At Mastery

Children who score at or above 90 percent

Following Assessment 15, Part A—Information

- Make seasons murals. Divide the class into four groups, and assign each group a season. Have children cut out magazine pictures or draw pictures appropriate to their season. Then have each group paste its pictures onto a large piece of paper to make a mural. Hang the murals on the walls of the classroom or in the hallways (Expanded Language Activities for lessons 141–145, page iv).
- Make a birthday calendar by using twelve large pieces of cardboard. Write the name of a month on each piece. Have children say the names of the months. Then ask each child to tell his or her birthday month. Group children according to the month of their birth. Give each group the cardboard labeled with their birth month, and have the group draw a picture of a birthday cake on its cardboard. After children complete the drawings, hang the birthday calendar on the wall (Expanded Language Activities for lessons 141–145, page iv).
- Play a kind of bingo game with objects form the different classes children have learned (tools, containers, buildings, food, and vehicles). Each child needs a bingo card and twenty pictures of objects. They may arrange the pictures any way they want. Then you call such directions as "Turn over all the furniture cards in the **N** column" or "Turn over all the vehicle cards in the **O** column" (Expanded Language Activities for lessons 146–150, page iv).

Following Assessment 15, Part B—Actions—Or

- Use the Actions Picture Cards to play What Am I Doing? Place all the cards upside down on a table. Allow one child to choose three cards. Have the child look at the cards and say to the class, "I am ___ ___ (insert the name of an action) **or** _____ (insert the name of a second action) **or** _____ (insert the name of the third action)." Then have the child perform or pantomime one of the actions. Allow the other children to guess the action and say the whole thing about what the child is doing. Repeat the game several times with different children and different actions (Picture Cards 1–9).

Enrichment Activities

- Play a version of Simon says that allows children to complete their choice of two or three actions. For example, say, "Simon says touch your head **or** touch your knees **or** touch your toes." Children may choose to touch either their head **or** knees **or** toes. Play several times using a variety of actions. Allow different children to play the role of Simon.

Following Assessment 15, Part C—Materials

- Play It's in the Bag. Select Picture Cards from the Furniture and Common Objects categories that match objects found in the classroom, such as desk, table, window, or door. Put the cards in a paper bag. Give children clues about the objects, including clues about the material from which each is made. Have children identify the object, including the material it is made from, and say the whole thing (Picture Cards User's Guide, page 10).
- Collect several types of materials such as cloth, rubber, wood, metal, paper, and leather. Using the house pattern from Build a House in Language Activity Masters Book 1, BLM 95A, have children attempt to make a house from all of the materials. Ask children why a house would be made of leather or cloth or rubber. Using the same materials and the Bear Hat pattern from Language Activity Masters Book 1, BLM 50, have children attempt to make a hat. Ask children why a hat would not be made of wood or metal. Allow the children to explain in their own words why certain objects are made of specific materials.

Following Assessment 15, Part D—Opposites

- Read *Where's My Teddy?* by Jez Alborough. Have children point out and describe things that are *big/small* opposites.
- Use Alligator Opposites (Language Activity Masters Book 2, lesson 130).

Following Assessment 15, Part E—Absurdities

- Use the How Absurd! Flip Book (Language Activity Masters Book 1, lesson 145).
- Read *And to Think That I Saw It on Mulberry Street!* by Dr. Seuss. Talk about what is absurd in the story.
- Read *If I Ran the Zoo,* by Dr. Seuss. Talk about what is absurd in the story.

Following Assessment 15, Part F—Rules

- Read "The Little Blue Bug," having children respond to questions about the rule in the story (Presentation Book D, Storybook 4, page 31).
- Have children make a picture book of classroom rules. For example, if the class has a "no running" rule, have children draw a picture of a child running in class with a circle around and slash through it. Beside that picture have children draw a picture of a child walking in class. Allow children to share their picture books with the class and describe the rules they have drawn.

Following Assessment 15, Part G—Same/Different

- Use Pack the Doctor's Bag. Modify the game to include picture cards of things that would go into a doctor's bag because they are the same (used by a doctor), and things that would not go into the bag because they are different (would not be used by a doctor) (Language Activity Masters Book 2, lesson 135).
- Play I'm Thinking of . . . Choose two or three objects that are either the same or different in some way. Give children clues about the objects that suggest how they are the same or different. The child who guesses the objects first can give the next clues. Play the game until all children have had an opportunity to give clues.

Following Assessment 15, Part H—Where, Who, When, What

- Use the Make Believe Menu (Language Activity Masters Book 1, lesson 150).
- Play the Order Up! Memory Game. Afterward, have children respond to *where, who, when,* and *what* questions about the activity (Language Activity Masters Book 2, lesson 150).
- Read "Dozy Delivers the Nails." Have children role-play the characters Dozy, Mr. Jackson, and the narrator, and have them respond to *where, who, when,* and *what* questions about the story (Presentation Book D, Storybook 4, page 25).

Tips for Teachers

English Language Learners

- See Extra Help guidelines for children who score below 90 percent or groups that average below 80 percent on Assessment 15.
- See Expanded Language Activities on page iv in Presentation Book D.
- Continue labeling classroom objects in English and, when available, in children's native languages.
- Show realia or other visuals of objects and concepts.
- Use TPR to model concepts by saying a word or phrase and then demonstrating the concept by pantomiming or gesturing. Guide children as they use TPR to demonstrate the concept.
- Have children cut out pictures from magazines or newspapers that show *who, what, where,* and *when.* Have children paste pictures on construction paper and share their stories.
- Have children add to their picture dictionaries by cutting out pictures from magazines or newspapers. Then play the You Be the Teacher game by having children take turns being the teacher and asking others "What does _____ mean?"
- Use primary language equivalents when available, and then ask children to say the words in English.

Home Connections

- Encourage children to share their completed workbook pages with their families.
- Provide an audiotape to use with picture flash cards of common objects, actions, and concepts taught.
- Provide a page of words for children to take home to practice "Sound it out; say it fast."
- Encourage children to practice mouth formations with a mirror at home.
- Encourage parents to help children practice using primary language equivalents and English words when possible.
- Encourage parents to read to their children or tell them a story using the pictures from the book, asking them what happened first, next, and last.
- Encourage parents to continue adding words their child is having difficulty with to his or her Word Wall. Then have parents take words their child has learned off the Word Wall.